MERRITT

A Canadian Before His Time

A Biography of
William Hamilton Merritt
by Jack Williams

© 1985
Stonehouse Publications
St. Catharines, Ontario, Canada

Author: Jack Williams

ISBN-0-919549-09-8

FIRST EDITION
Copyright 1985 Stonehouse Publications

Published by:
Stonehouse Publications
17 Queen Street
St. Catharines, Ontario, Canada
L2R 5G5

TABLE OF CONTENTS

ILLUSTRATIONS

Chapter One

YOUNG MERRITT

William Hamilton Merritt was stubborn; or, as one of his contemporaries more politely described him, "single-minded." Once possessed of an idea — and he had many — it became all-consuming. Even his family, strong as his ties with them were, had time and again to take second place to the cause he was pursuing at the moment.

One of the strongest motivating forces in his life was an ambition to be successful in business; though his commercial affairs were frequently in jeopardy, several times he was on the verge of bankruptcy. He appeared to find his greatest satisfaction in accomplishment: in the stupendous feat of constructing the first canal linking the St. Lawrence with the upper lakes, in the bridging of the turbulent Niagara River, or in the attainment of political objectives. The real significance of his accomplishments can only be appreciated fully when they are measured against the background of the times, under conditions extremely difficult compared to present day circumstances.

Canada has been described as a country which came into existence and survives despite its geography. Few countries are as dependent on transportation for their very existence; and it was here that Merritt made his greatest contribution. In his earlier days there were no railways, and the only roads were rudimentary cuttings through the forests, impassable when the weather was unfavourable. The only dependable means of transport was by water, making the building of the Welland Canal, for which Merritt was responsible, essential to the preservation of the Canadian identity and the opening of the Canadian west.

He was a man of many contradictions. While he might properly be described as conservative, he was seldom swayed by convention. A devout member of the Church of England, he had greater admiration for the

1

Methodist Church. In politics he differed openly with some of his party's policies and resigned a ministerial portfolio in protest. An avowed capitalist and a strong believer in free enterprise, he pressed for the establishment of a central bank, government-owned and controlled. As an entrepreneur he defied public ridicule of his enterprises.

This spirit of dogged determination and individualism was responsible for the indelible mark he left on the important period when Canada was emerging from pioneering agriculture into a more complex society. Still more important was his contribution to what was to become a typically Canadian blending of private and public enterprise, still a contemporary approach to the problems of some Canadian industries.

The Merritt family came to Canada by force of circumstances. They had resided in Westchester County, near New York City, at the time of the American Revolution. Staunchly loyal to the Crown, Thomas Merritt, the father of William Hamilton Merritt, enlisted in the Queen's Rangers under the command of Colonel John Graves Simcoe. When the regiment went south Thomas Merritt met and married Mary Hamilton of South Carolina. Later the regiment returned north and the young couple took up residence near New York, where the Queen's Rangers disbanded in 1783.

The loyalist members of the Merritt family were uncomfortable in the post-revolutionary atmosphere of the new republic and they moved to New Brunswick. But there they found the winter too cold, and so they returned to her home in South Carolina. These were difficult days for the couple, Mrs. Merritt had suffered a miscarriage. They finally decided to go back to the Merritt family home at Bedford, N.Y. There William Hamilton Merritt was born, 3 July 1793.

But they were still unsettled and Thomas Merritt became interested in efforts being made by his old commanding officer, Simcoe, to settle the newly-created province of Upper Canada. Simcoe had been appointed Lieutenant-Governor and had revived the Queen's Rangers, enlisting some of his wartime comrades to assist in establishing the new province and its capital.

In 1794 Thomas Merritt went to Niagara (Niagara-on-the-Lake), which Simcoe had renamed Newark, to investigate the possibilities of settlement. Simcoe gave him a warm welcome which so impressed him that a few months later, in 1796, with his young family he moved to Upper Canada, thus qualifying as a United Empire Loyalist. William Hamilton Merritt thereby became the son of a Loyalist.

It was a difficult journey. In most of the country through which they had to pass there were no roads. Travel had to be by paths through the forest, or, preferably, by water. The territory was largely inhabited by Indians, whose attitude toward white men, and particularly strangers, was highly uncertain. The route the Merritts followed by sloop up the Hudson River to Albany; then by smaller craft — the bateau — up the Mohawk to Oswego on Lake Ontario. The bateau was the water work horse of the time, varying in size from a large rowboat to a small barge. Flat-bottomed they might be thirty or forty feet in length with a beam of five to eight feet. Benches accommodated both passengers and the oarsmen who provided the motive power, supplemented at times by small sails, or in shallow water by poles. One of the advantages of the bateau was that it could navigate shallow water, though at times the passengers were required to get out to lighten the load. Travel was at the pace of about three miles an hour, or thirty miles a day.

Part of the price settlers had to pay for their new life in Upper Canada was the sacrifice of many of their worldly possessions. They were able to keep what they could take with them on their journey north.

On his earlier visit Merritt had seen maps indicating the land available for settlers; but when he returned with his family he found most of the more attractive sites had already been claimed. This was particularly true of land along the Niagara River, largely occupied by former members of Butler's Rangers, who qualified for free land as a reward for their services in the Revolutionary War. When the Merritt family arrived plans to move the provincial capital from Newark across the lake to York (Toronto) were well advanced and free land was being offered to attract settlers to the north shore of Lake Ontario.

But Merritt had planned to make his new home in the Niagara District, and that was still what he wanted. Land between the Niagara River and Burlington at the head of the lake — in essence the whole of the Niagara District — had been purchased by the British under the terms of a treaty with the Indians in 1792. Merritt was attracted by a location which appeared on the maps to be a small river a few miles from the Niagara River. He was told it was known as the Twelve Mile Creek, so named because of its distance from the mouth of the Niagara. Land was available there, but only for purchase. Merritt bought 200 acres in a location which eventually became the City of St. Catharines.

The life of pioneer settlers was hard. The area was heavily wooded with pine, oak, walnut and other varieties. Land had to be cleared and a log house built. Crops had to be planted. The fruit trees, for which the Niagara District was to become famous, were just being introduced.

Prices can be misleading; but those prevailing at the turn of the century can be related to a farm worker's wage of 50 cents a day. Flour was $7.50 a hundred weight; salt, $4.50 a bushel; deer skins, 63 cents; bear skins, $2.50; rum, $3 a gallon; candles, 30 cents a pound; calico, 18 cents a yard; and a spinning wheel could be bought for $6.

The staple foods were pork, flour, potatoes and corn, supplemented by a plentiful supply of fish and game. But these had not always been available. When the Merritts arrived the settlers were still talking of "The Hungry Year" of 1788-9. That had been a period when scorching heat and drought left many families near the starvation level. Livestock died, game disappeared, springs and wells dried, leaving only those near the lake with access to water.

Without the normal supply of food families had tried boiling tree bark. Years later they told of watching what the pigs ate in order to determine which wild roots were not poisonous. It was a time that called for courage and suffering for those trying to establish a new home.

Supplies had been made available from the King's stores — the army stock at Niagara — but these were insufficient to meet the needs. Later some overly-officious officers tried to collect from the settlers for the goods they had received. When Prince Edward visited Niagara in 1791 a delegation of the settlers, who were said to be in debt to the King, waited on him. On

3

behalf of his father Prince Edward ordered the debts cancelled.

Despite the disaster of "The Hungry Year" the population grew. Much of the activity was along the Niagara River. The portage around Niagara Falls was the key to the route to the west, and the only means of overcoming the hurdle presented by the falls and the rapids, a barrier later to be successfully challenged by the Welland Canal. The shortest portage route lay on the American side of the river, and after the Revolution it was considered essential to develop a route on Canadian soil. An Indian trail already existed and with the growth of settlements along the river increased use of paths connecting the clearings finally developed into something resembling a road.

In 1788 an army engineer recommended the construction of permanent wharfing facilities at Queenston on the lower Niagara River, with a proper road from there to Chippawa above the Falls. From that point the river was navigable to Lake Erie, despite a strong current. A group of traders, headed by Robert Hamilton, a Queenston merchant, was already using the route to convey trading goods west and move furs east.

Teams of up to five oxen, or two to four span of horses, hauled heavily built wagons with barrels, boxes and sacks of merchandise over the portage. When the government undertook the construction and maintenance of a permanent road Hamilton and his associates won the contract.

Warehouses were built, as well as accommodation for the troops stationed at Queenston on guard duty. Mrs. Simcoe, wife of the Governor, wrote in her dairy of a trip from Newark to Niagara Falls and described the road as "tolerable", despite a number of stumps remaining. It obviously left a good deal to be desired for on another occasion she told of driving the carriage herself, with her four-year-old son, Francis, being tied in and "much bruised and shook."

By the time the Merritts settled in the area a stage coach carried mail three times a week between Newark and Chippawa. Queenston — named after the Queen's Rangers stationed there — had become a bustling commercial centre. One visitor told of seeing four vessels of from 60 to 100 tons unloading at the wharf where there might be as many as sixty wagons a day.

A rudimentary road which ran from Niagara to Burlington, at the western end of Lake Ontario, passed by the Merritt's new home. The settlement there became known as Shipman's Corners, named after Paul Shipman who operated a tavern there. This road followed an Indian trail with a rough bridging of the Twelve Mile Creek. Mrs. Simcoe regarded it with even less favour than the Portage Road, speaking of it as "a most terrible road . . . full of stumps, fallen trees, etc.", adding that horses "plunged to their knees in pools half full of logs."

By 1799 a small log schoolhouse had been built at Shipman's Corners and there William Hamilton Merritt began his formal education. At the same time he was receiving some practical education at home, being assigned at an early age the chilling task of lighting the morning fire. Later he was entrusted with driving loads of wheat to the grist mill — the beginning of a career as a miller.

Thomas Merritt clearly had ambitions for his son; no sooner had he

4

exhausted the educational facilities at Shipman's Corners than he was sent off to Ancaster where Richard Cockerell, one of the provinces leading educators, had a school. It is significant that there Merritt learned something of the rudiments of land surveying. While he was at Ancaster his father gave him a pony, enabling him to both improve his horsemanship and become familiar with the geography of the area. These attributes were to prove highly useful to young Merritt and his country a few years later.

Before long Cockerell moved his school to Niagara where Hamilton also received instruction in the classics from the local Presbyterian minister, the Rev. John Burns. Being at Niagara widened the scope of the lad's experience and outlook. His father had been appointed sheriff of the district in 1803; and in that capacity had frequent occasion to visit Niagara where the Merritts became well known and respected.

While the capital had been moved to York, Niagara remained an important centre of military, legal and commercial activity, providing the nucleus of an elite social circle, described by William Kirby in his "Annals of Niagara" as "men of education and civil and military experience." Frequent parties and balls, as well as amusements for the population at large, made for an active social life. Indian lacrosse games attracted large crowds, as did horse racing and military displays on the commons. There young Merritt had his first contact with the army in which he was to serve much sooner than he anticipated.

In 1808, Hamilton having reached the age of fifteen, his father thought he should go still further afield. Thomas Merritt enlisted the co-operation of his brother, Nehemiah Merritt of Saint John, N.B., a successful businessman engaged in various enterprises, including shipping. The senior Merritts arranged to have Hamilton go to Quebec City where he would board his uncle's ship "Lord Sheffield" and sail to Halifax. From there he was to go to Saint John to continue his education.

And so Hamilton set out on what must have been, for those times, an adventurous journey. It developed into an experience that would be exciting in any age. He travelled by schooner down Lake Ontario to Kingston, then by bateau to Montreal; again by schooner from there to Three Rivers; and finally by hired caleche to Quebec City. There the "Lord Sheffield" was taking on cargo for a voyage to the West Indies. Hamilton was welcomed by his uncle who showed him the sights of the city and outfitted him with sailor's clothing.

Then they sailed. Once they reached the open water of the Gulf of St. Lawrence young Merritt suffered from seasickness; but it soon passed and before the ship reached Halifax he was able to learn something of the elements of sailing.

Outside the British Isles the east coast port of Halifax was the British navy's most important base, and with Britain at war with France it was a hive of activity. Merritt had his first glimpse of the majesty of large naval vessels and he was indirectly affected by a naval custom of the day. Three members of the "Lord Sheffield's" crew were impressed for naval service. Nehemiah Merritt was able to have them freed, but decided the ship should leave port as quickly as possible to avoid further complications.

Another difficulty arose however. One of the officers proved to be an alcoholic and unfit for duty. Nehemiah suggested to his nephew that he postpone going to Saint John and join the crew with the rank of supercargo, looking after the cargo and commercial matters. It takes a little imagination to realize the enthusiasm with which a fifteen-year-old boy would accept such an invitation.

But he little knew what he was in for. Soon after sailing from Halifax the ship ran into a series of gales. The weather became so severe that lumber being carried on the deck had to be jettisoned. The vessel sprang a leak and for a time it was thought she would have to put in at Charleston; but the weather improved and she was able to proceed to the Bermudas, finally docking at the Island of St. George.

The voyage had taken five weeks; but even worse was to come. Soon after her arrival the island was struck by a hurricane, so severe that the "Lord Sheffield" broke her mooring and drifted ashore. When she was finally returned to the dock an inspection showed her to be so badly damaged that she was declared unseaworthy and had to be sold.

Hamilton Merritt and his uncle were stranded; but under the circumstances which proved not unpleasant. Nehemiah Merritt had business connections who entertained them during a six week stay on the island.

Finally, in late December 1808, they obtained passage on a ship bound for New York, and for a fare of $50 each they were able to start home. The voyage took only twelve days.

At Saint John, Hamilton resumed his studies in a variety of subjects, ranging from bookkeeping to Latin, and including navigation, surveying and mathematics. He gained some practical experience in land surveying and gained an insight into his uncle's business, visiting fishing grounds and fish processing plants.

Not all was work however. Saint John was noted for its attractive young women and Hamilton, at sixteen, had reached an age when such matters aroused his interest. He found the social graces he had learned at Niagara useful. In his diary he referred to the number of attractive young women in the community: "very handsome, fresh, brisk, rosy and delicate." They were fond of outdoor exercise and "glad to see young fellows of an evening to chat with, as beaux are somewhat scarce." He took advantage of the social life and went "strawberrying" and even to a quilting bee, which he found "very delightful."

By autumn, however, he decided it was time to go home. He travelled by ship to New York, adding to his seagoing adventures when the ship ran aground at Martha's Vineyard. He spent several days in New York, seeing something of life in a big city, and then proceeded by boat up the Hudson River to Albany. There he purchased a horse and rode to Lewiston, N.Y., crossing the Niagara River by ferry and arriving home just in time for the family Christmas dinner. He had spent the year 1809 in Saint John and on the long journey home.

While he had been away the little community at Shipman's Corners had grown. It was thought time for him to settle down to work and a partnership was purchased for him in a general store operated by William Chisholm. The store served the area, relieving families of the necessity of travelling to Niagara for their supplies.

Typical of the general stores of the day, most of the goods were obtained from Montreal, the wholesale source for merchants throughout the country. Cash was extremely scarce and most of the business was done by trade or barter. All kinds of produce - honey, pork, fruit, as well as lumber, hides and ashes for the production of potash used in the manufacture of soap, were traded for merchandise. These products the merchants shipped to Montreal. The transactions necessitated a complicated system of bookkeeping and Merritt expressed the opinion that most of the commercial failures were attributable to a lack of sound knowledge of the subject; though events were to prove that his own skill in bookkeeping was limited.

Before long young Merritt became restless, apparently finding the life of a merchant too confining. Throughout his life he displayed a liking for the freedom of outdoor activities. At the same time his services were needed at home. His father's responsibilities as sheriff left him little time for the family farm; and so Hamilton sold his interest in the store and took over management of the farm, as well as some nearby leased land. With the proceeds from the sale of his interest in the store he purchased horses, cattle and farm implements, and soon had 200 acres under cultivation.

Thus, at the age of nineteen, William Hamilton Merritt had experienced something of the life of pioneer settlers, had sailed the Atlantic and faced its hazards, had engaged in retail trade and has operated a sizeable farm.

But a still more exciting future was in store.

Colonel John Graves Simcoe

8

Sir Isaac Brock

9

Gage House, Stoney Creek Battle

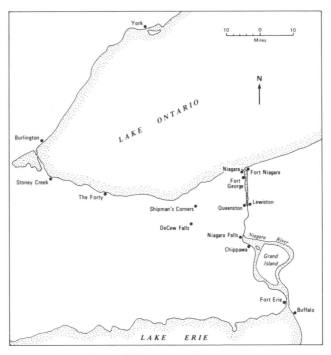

Map of Niagara, Circa 1812

Chapter Two

THE SOLDIER

Hamilton Merritt's immediate and intense involvement in the War of 1812 was natural. A strong military tradition went far back in his family, including his father's service in the Revolutionary War. The family had moved to Canada because, true to their loyalist sentiments, they preferred living under the Union Jack. Now the new life they had chosen was being challenged.

British North America, with a population of less than 500,000 was being threatened by the United States with a population of 7,500,000. In all Canada the permanent army numbered less than 5,000; and although trained and disciplined such a force was pathetically inadequate to defend such a large expanse of territory. The permanent army needed the support of the local militia and Indians. The Militia Act required all ablebodied males to render military service as members of the militia. The only exemptions were on religious grounds, and then there was a penalty to be paid. But Merritt had freely volunteered for service before the outbreak of war and held a commission as a Lieutenant.

The war was not unexpected. The formal declaration came in Washington 19 June 1812, and the news reached Upper Canada eight days later. The province was under the administration of General Sir Isaac Brock, a British career officer. Brock received the news at York and hastened across the lake to Fort George at Niagara, directly on the frontier, where action might be expected.

At the same time young Merritt was at Shipman's Corners. He hurried to Fort George and reported to Brock personally. The general had a low opinion of the Canadian militia, as well as a distaste for colonial life in general; but this seems not to have extended to Merritt. The young officer idolized the general who, despite his dislikes, was a highly popular figure in Niagara's social circles.

Brock immediately assigned Merritt a party of twenty men and despatched him to Chippawa on the Niagara River, just above the Falls, to perform guard duty. There his squad was doubled. The nineteen-year-old officer was already experiencing something of military responsibility. An invasion from the American side was expected momentarily, and the men took their duties very seriously.

Merritt was proud of the response of his little group of amateur soldiers. Poorly trained and ill equipped as they were, they faced the enemy with courage and determination. In an entirely new role they patrolled the shore of the river, developing a sense of discipline. Batteries were erected at key locations and officers rode busily to and fro checking the posts. It was a far cry from the peaceful life of a Niagara farm, but the men were quick to adapt.

This was the beginning of what was to prove a significant period in Merritt's life. His father had also reported for duty and had been given charge of the cavalry with the rank of major.

The anticipated attack across the river failed to materialize and the constant guard duty became monotonous; but Merritt's first taste of military service in time of war was very different from what was to come. Apart from the military aspect there are suggestions that it was at this time, constantly watching Niagara's waters, that he first conceived the idea of a canal to circumvent Niagara Falls. He can hardly have helped being impressed by the endless flow of such a volume of water.

As the days went by and the anticipated invasion failed to materialize it was decided to allow a number of the miltiamen to go home to take in their crops. Merritt, however, was kept on duty and it was a month before he was granted leave to visit his home, only fifteen miles distant. When he finally arrived home he found almost the entire crop destroyed. Only a portion had been saved by an old pensioner who had tried to help Merritt's mother preserve something of the farm. This debacle marked a sudden end to Merrit's career in agriculture and he noted in his diary that: "I never worked a day at that occupation again." Another episode in his already crowded life had ended.

He had been home only a few hours when new orders arrived, directly from Brock. There had been important developments to the west and the Detroit-Amherstburg area had become a focal point in the war. Brock was going there to assume personal command and he instructed Merritt to take steps to maintain the lines of communication between Amherstburg and York.

A postscript to the general's message made clear Merritt's standing with Brock: "I am well pleased with your exertions, and wish you to see more active service."

On his way to carry out this mission Merritt came upon a group of American sympathizers. The young officer and his men, lacking distinctive uniforms, posed as "Yankees" and, as a result "the people discovered their sentiments to us, so I made a dozen of them prisoners." Merritt took two of the party back to Fort George and later reported to Brock who, he found, was "well pleased with my proceedings," Looking after the prisoners had delayed him and Merritt did not arrive until the day after Detroit had fallen to the British. Nevertheless, he was awarded the special Detroit Medal, struck to commemorate the engagement.

This experience marked a turning point in his life as a soldier. He found there was more to fighting a war than routine sentry duty. His participation in the Detroit campaign, which had given him the opportunity to exercise personal initiative, had a lasting effect on his character.

The personality that emerged was very different from the sombre faced politician-entrepreneur depicted in later portraits of the Hon. William Hamilton Merritt, M.P. This was a dashing cavalry officer, riding day and night and engaging in guerrilla-type warfare. He gloried in nipping at the heels of a retreating enemy, staging hit-and run raids on enemy outposts, posing as an American to flush out spies and informers, protecting settlers' families from marauding parties, stealing American horses. Constantly, through all these adventures, there was a burning determination to settle a personal score with one particular individual on the American side — Joseph Willcocks — of whom more was to be heard.

Merritt fought beside his father at the Battle of Queenston Heights, where Major Merritt had the honour of collecting the swords of the American officers. Thomas Merritt's stature was further recognized when he was chosen one of the pall bearers at the funeral of the beloved Brock, who had fallen mortally wounded in the battle. Years later Hamilton Merritt was active in arranging for the erection of a monument at Queenston in recognition of Brock.

Despite hard-fought battles the war went through periods of relative quiet, during which members of the militia were temporarily released from duty and allowed to return home to look after their farms. This was the situation in late February 1813, when Merritt was instructed to raise a troop of cavalry, which he would command with the rank of captain. The task was not easy; the volunteers were expected to provide their own horses and other equipment. However, two weeks later he had forty men available and they were once again assigned to guard duty along the Niagara River where an invasion was expected.

That failed to materialize; but Fort George, where Merritt was, came under heavy cannonading from Fort Niagara on the American side. The fort soon caught fire and Merritt complained that a shortage of ammunition prevented return of the fire. The American fleet had been off Niagara for several days and on the morning of 27 May 1813, under the protection of a heavy fog, a landing was effected.

The British force of 800 was pushed back and the Americans occupied what was left of Fort George. The British retreated all the way to Burlington at the head of the lake. Merritt, with his little troop, did their best to protect the rear of the retreating army, engaging in several skirmishes and incurring a number of casualties.

The situation had become desperate. Brock's death had been a catastrophe, his leadership was sorely missed. While the British retreat had been at least temporarily halted at Burlington, the future of the whole of Upper Canada hung in the balance. Withdrawal from Burlington meant falling back to York, which was already in partial ruin as the result of an earlier attack by the Americans. After York the course of retreat would have to be to Kingston, leaving almost the whole of the province in American hands.

The main body of the militia had been disbanded; but Merritt, still

13

under orders, became involved in sporadic actions which cost the lives of several of his men. He became deeply depressed and wrote in his dairy:

> I feel in a sad dilemma - the thought of abandoning the country, leaving everything that was near and dear to me, was most depressing; still more so the unhappy situation of my family, whom we left unprotected. My father, knowing the insults he would be subject to if he remained, determined to follow the army. For me there was no alternative, or I should certainly have remained behind to protect my mother and sisters.

These was trying days for the people of the Niagara District. Territory changed hands time and again. With the British forces at Burlington, the whole of the peninsula was occupied by the Americans. Indians and renegade bands of soldiers frequently looted and burned farm homes. Most of the able-bodied men were on military duty and frequently only the women and the elderly were left to protect the property. Some families doubled up for their own safety and farm properties were left vacant.

On some occasions settlers suffered from the actions of their own forces in the commandeering of supplies. An example was the experience of George Adams, a magistrate at the Twelve Mile Creek and a friend of the Merrit's. He had served with the Lincoln Militia until he was seriously wounded. At one point General John Vincent, advancing with the British forces, used the Adams residence as his headquarters, making free use of the family's possessions. Adams later submitted an account for losses totalling £98.50.0, which, among other items, included: "48 sheep killed and carried away by troops of Indians under the command of General Vincent. 37 fat hogs taken from my Distillery. One horse wagon (sic) taken by Dr. Thomas for the use of the hospital, never returned."

Later, when the British withdrew, Adams became a prisoner of the Americans and his distillery was destroyed.

The Merritt family suffered from these conditions and at times had to leave their home for safer surroundings. On one occasion Hamilton Merritt was reprimanded by a superior officer for taking time to transport his ailing father to Burlington. His mother refused to move, saying she had become used to invasions.

Later Thomas Merritt was taken prisoner and held at Fort Niagara. His captor was the peculiar character Joseph Willcocks, who at one time had been a member of the Upper Canada Assembly, but who had gone over to the American side. An Irishman, he had emigrated to Canada in 1799, quickly establishing himself at York where he was made sheriff. His radical views were responsible for his dismissal a few years later. For a time he published a newspaper—UPPER CANADIAN GUARDIAN OR FREEMAN'S JOURNAL— at Niagara. He was elected to the House of Assembly but spent the first part of his term in jail for libelling the House to which he had been elected.

His services were briefly used by Brock in seeking Indian support and it is believed he fought with the British in the Battle of Queenston Heights. But his loyalty changed when he became frustrated with the political attacks to which he was subjected. He crossed to the United States and undertook the formation of a military unit which he named "The Canadian Volunteers."

He used his knowledge of the Niagara District to advantage, and with small roving bands sought revenge on those he regarded as his political enemies. In this connection he seized the senior Merritt and turned him over to American authorities, thereby arousing bitter and unforgiving anger on the part of Hamilton Merritt.

The Americans appear not to have shared Willcocks' feelings toward Thomas Merritt. It was the practice of opposing armies to exchange communications by means of messages carried by an officer under a flag of truce - a white flag. This was sometimes little more than an attempt to learn something of conditions behind the enemy's lines. While Thomas Merritt was being held at Fort Niagara, Hamilton Merritt was sent on such a mission to Fort George, then held by the Americans. He was blindfolded and taken to the American commanding officer, General William Henry Harrison, who obligingly sent across the river and had Thomas Merritt brought to the Canadian side so he might see his son. Assurance was given that he would soon be released, and he was.

But the memory of Willcocks' treatment of his father lingered with Hamilton Merritt, and he became obsessed with the idea of reprisal. As he rode the district he was constantly on the lookout, hopeful of capturing Willcocks. He wrote of "having taken many a long ride, in the lonely hours of the night, in the hope of catching Wilcox (sic) and making an example of him and all traitors." William Kirby, a Niagara historian with a colourful style, described Willcocks as "a tonguey, tricky, unscrupulous, bad living fellow" who joined the Americans and "fought for them, robbed, stole, burned and murdered for them."

Merritt continued his pursuit of Willcocks with a passion and hatred that ran deep; but he was never successful in catching him. Neither did Willcocks escape; he was killed in action at Fort Erie 4 October 1814. But not before he had taken his revenge on the people of Niagara by burning their buildings.

Historic events tend to become embellished with time, but there can have been no more bizarre engagement in the War of 1812 than that which took place at Stoney Creek, and in which Hamilton Merritt was deeply involved. The Americans had been slow to take advantage of their victory at Fort George and the subsequent British retreat to Burlington. The 700-odd British regulars, with some militia, were being pursued at a leisurely pace by an American force of 3,000. Shortly after the British stopped at Burlington the Americans made camp at Stoney Creek, about seven miles distant.

Just a few miles from Burlington was Dundas where soldiers would go when the opportunity offered to escape temporarily from military discipline and the discomforts of army life. This was particularly true of Merritt whose sister, Caroline-Matilda (Mrs. James Gordon) lived there.

Among the members of the 49th Regiment encamped at Burlington was Lieutenant James FitzGibbon, a soldier who had been a favourite of Brock's and with whom Merritt was to form a close association. FitzGibbon disguised himself as a peddler and crossed the American lines offering butter for sale. He was able to gauge the size and deployment of the American force and became convinced that a surprise attack might well succeed. He carried this information back and urged the British commanding officer, General John Vincent, to take the offensive.

The chance of success increased when the American password was learned. Merritt had just arrived back from dinner with his sister when, about midnight, the troops sleeping on the grass were wakened. Flints were removed from their rifles to prevent accidental firing which might make their presence known. Silently they moved off in the darkness. Merritt was with them, attached to General Vincent's staff.

At three in the morning they reached the first American sentry at Stoney Creek. He was bayoneted. Nearby a group of Americans were found sleeping in a church. They were taken prisoner.

Then came the major assault; the attackers, whooping like Indians in an attempt to frighten the sleepy-eyed American soldiers. Bedlam broke loose. Merritt described it as "the greatest disorder and confusion imagineable." American guns opened fire from an advantageous position on a hill. First the American line gave way, then the British.

Only the flash of gunfire lit the night. In hand-to-hand combat it became difficult to identify friend from foe. The two senior American officers - Brigadier General John Chandler and Brigadier General William Winder - blundered into the British lines and were both taken prisoner. General Vincent lost his horse and wandered off into the forest. Things became so confused that each side thought the other had won the day. Lieutenant John Harvey, who had assumed command of the British force, ordered a withdrawal.

With daylight it was decided an attempt should be made to determine General Vincent's fate, and the task was assigned to Merritt, who later recorded a first-hand account:

After we left the field, Col. Harvey desired me to return and if possible find Maj. Gen. Vincent, supposed to be either dead or wounded. Not thinking of the enemy I was challenged by a sentry under old Gage's house. I was on the point of surrendering, as my pistols were both in my holsters, when I adopted the strategy of enquiring who placed him there?' and rode up to him. He, by my blue coat, took me for one of his own party, and answered his captain, who had just gone into the house with a party of men.' I then enquired if they had found the British general, and pulled out my pistol, which made him drop his gun. At that moment a man without any gun ran down the hill; I called him; he came, when I had the good fortune to secure both and bring them off. This stratagem had succeeded once before or I should not have thought of it.

General Vincent was finally found wandering in the woods, lost but unharmed.

Harvey had withdrawn the British troops, thinking his position would become untenable if the Americans discovered he had barely 700 men. But the Americans were equally anxious to avoid further engagement and they hurriedly moved back to the Forty Mile Creek (Grimsby). Their retreat was so hasty that tents were left standing and some of the wounded and dead lay where they had fallen. This was the scene the British found when they returned and took over the field early in the afternoon.

But even in retreat the Americans were not safe. British naval vessels appeared off the Forty Mile Creek and began bombarding the American encampment. The Americans then withdrew to Fort George, with the British in pursuit. The tide of war had turned and the force that had been retreating was now on the offensive and had regained occupation of the Niagara Peninsula.

Opportunities increased for Merritt and his troop to engage in freelance activities. The fact that they spoke the same language and that their clothing was nondescript, gave them considerable latitude in hunting "Yankee sympathizers".

Merritt shared these adventures with FitzGibbon, the officer who had penetrated the enemy lines at Stoney Creek. FitzGibbon had been given a troop of fifty men who were equipped not only with their own uniforms, but also with jackets they could use to disguise themselves as Americans. They became adept at scattering to give the impression of numbers far beyond their actual strength; and they exchanged signals and passed orders by the tinkling of cow bells. These men were vital to the lines of communication. On one occasion Merritt rode a distance of a hundred miles in nine-and-a-half hours.

This was the type of warfare that suited him and his men. Ernest Green, in "The Niagara Portage Road", speaks of the "the dash and daring of FitzGibbon and Merritt's troopers", continuing:

Many a stirring tale has been told of the wild doing along the road in that leafy June when the bloody boys' hung upon the invaders' flanks, cutting off their scouts, seized their spies, raided their wagon trains and pulled up bridges to check pursuit. Merritt and FitzGibbon dashed that way through the night into the country behind Fort Erie to seize suspected spies and traitors, bringing their prisoners in through the very lines of the foe.

On another occasion General Jacob Brown marched a sizeable force down the River Road to encompass Fort George. As soon as he was out of sight of Queenston FitzGibbon and Merritt, with a band of thirty chosen cavalrymen, dashed into the village and captured some prisoners. They later went down the road to "tweak the dragon's tail." Merritt told of his little band keeping a party of 150 dragoons at bay until they were completely outflanked. They enjoy nothing more than hanging on to the skirts of the enemy and making a nuisance of themselves. Five or six times a day they, would engage in these brief but spirited engagements.

The base for many of these excursions into enemy territory was the DeCew House, near Beaver Dams. This provided control of several roads, and at the same time the large stone residence was used both as army headquarters and a military hospital. It became the key location in the famed Laura Secord story and the Battle of Beaver Dams.

The Americans determined to take this strategic position and curb the troublesome and evasive young cavalrymen, assigned Lieutenant Colonel Charles Boerstler with a force of 600 men. At Queenston Laura Secord overheard the officers discussing their plans, and she set out on the long and arduous walk to DeCew to warn FitzGibbon. John Norton, one of the most competent Indian leaders and a careful observer, explained what happened:

> On the evening of the second day, a loyal inhabitant brought information that the enemy intended to attack us that night with six hundred men. We therefore moved from our quarters, and dressed an ambuscade on the side of the road by which the enemy had to pass - but this precaution proved to be premature, he had not yet sufficiently prepared to assail us.

According to Norton, a party of Indians searching for a young Caughnawaga, who was missing, quite by accident came in sight of the American force, 600 strong. The Indians quickly gathered more Indian warriors, attacked the Americans two miles from FitzGibbon's position, and forced them to surrender, 24 June 1813. In his first account of the battle, FitzGibbon, then a Lieutenant in the 49th Regiment, took credit for the victory. Merritt, in his JOURNAL, quoted Norton, who had the ability to express himself well, in one sentence: "The Cognauga (sic) Indians fought the battle, the Mohawks got the plunder and FitzGibbon got the credit." To Merritt went the responsibility of escorting the 600 prisoners to the Forty Mile Creek where a British base camp had been established.

Captain William Kerr, who led the Mohawks in the battle, was rightfully annoyed by FitzGibbon's biased account. In a memorial, written after the war, Kerr put the record straight and FitzGibbon, on 30 March 1818, was forced to admit:

> With respect to the affair with Captin Boerstler, not a shot was fired on our side by any but the Indians. They beat the American detachment into a state of terror, and the only share I claim is taking advantage of a favourable moment to offer them protection from the tomahawk and scalping knife. The Indian Department did all the rest.

The conditions under which the troops were fighting were at times pitiful. Exposure, lack of efficient commissariat and shortages of medical supplies took a heavy toll in fever and other illnesses among the officers and men of both the permanent force and the militia.

James Fulton, aide to Sir George Prevost, describing conditions experienced by troops in the Niagara Peninsula in the summer of 1813, wrote of finding troops "in great distress for the necessities: shorts, shoes and stockings. Many of the men of the 49th are literally naked." And about the same time General Francis de Rottenburg reported the 49th Regiment to be "in rags and without shoes."

Merritt spent part of the summer of 1813 on a trip to Montreal in an effort to obtain much needed clothing and equipment, including bridles and saddles. He left for Montreal late in July and at Kingston came in contact with British forces and their commander-in-chief, Sir George Prevost, to whom he was presented. The experience left a lasting and unfortunate impression. When Merritt spoke of his mission he was told bluntly that the war was nearing an end and there appeared little further need for the services of his troop. A shocked Merritt immediately submitted his resignation, but it was refused. He went on to Montreal; but with a new and less favourable opinion of his commander-in-chief, and a realization that in the regular force there was little regard for the militia, except in times of dire need.

However, at Montreal he was well received by Sir Roger Sheaffe, who had fought at Queenston Heights, and by his aide, Captain Loring, who also knew Merritt. He obtained some clothing, but was unable to get other equipment, even though he waited three weeks in the hope of new supplies arriving from England. He finally returned, reaching home 20 September.

There he found a discouraging situation. The morale of both soldiers and civilians was in a sad state. Merritt set about reorganizing his troop and again resorted to guerrilla tactics to replace some of the horses. He discarded those considered imperfect and replaced them at the expense of the enemy by making unexpected forays and carrying off their best beasts.

During the whole of the war few, if any, events so moved Merritt as did the destruction of the Town of Niagara. On the night of 10 December 1813 at the Twelve Mile Creek he saw a glare in the sky. The whole of the Town of Niagara was ablaze. He later described the scene that confronted him when he arrived at the former provincial capital:

> Nothing but heaps of coal and the streets full of furniture that the inhabitants had been fortunate enought to get out of their homes, met the eye in all directions. Mr. Gordon's house, my old quarters, was the only one left standing. The Garrison was abandoned. Many tents left standing, the barracks and woodwork nearly consumed. We were very apprehensive that a mine was left for our destruction; a musket cartridge burst upon our ascending the cavalier bastion. Each took it for a match to a concealed mine, and gave up our lives for a ride in the air, fortunately our fears were groundless.

Merritt's old enemy Willcocks had been on hand as the senior officer on the staff of George McClure, the American commanding officer. When the Americans decided to abandon Fort George and the Town of Niagara the inhabitants were given only a few minutes notice before their homes were set afire. Little could be saved and the burning extended to homes along the River Road toward Queenston.

The British were determined to get revenge and Merritt was assigned to arrange for teams of horses to haul boats from as far distant as Burlington for a crossing of the Niagara River. Before he could complete the task he collapsed from exhaustion and was taken by sleigh to his home. As a result he was deprived of, as he put it, "sharing in the most glorious affair that happened in the Upper Province."

A British force of 500 regulars crossed the river and took Fort Niagara without a shot being fired. Other troops and a band of Indians followed and soon they were burning the Village of Lewiston. A few days later another force crossed above Niagara Falls, with 1,500 regulars and Indians. They set fire to buildings at Black Rock and Buffalo, as well as destroying four schooners and extensive supplies.

Washington was quick to deny responsibility for McClure's action at Niagara, and Sir George Prevost issued a proclamation expressing his disapproval of the retaliatory response by the British troops. Both armies had vented their feelings; but it was the inhabitants on both sides of the river who were the victims.

19

Throughout the war periods of violence and suffering continued to alternate with social activities that were almost normal. At one stage, while he was stationed at St. Davids, Merritt complained that he had little to do "except taking tea with the ladies." But such gatherings were only brief interludes in a deadly conflict. This was no war of tea and crumpets; soldiers met violent death, others suffered horrible wounds and received only the crudest medical attention.

The Battle of Chippawa Creek, 5 July 1814, was an example. Two days prior Merritt had been at home with his family and friends who had gathered to celebrate his twenty-first birthday. They were just sitting down to dinner in the late afternoon when word arrived that the Americans had made a successful crossing at Fort Erie. Merritt left immediately to report to his headquarters at Fort George. There he found his commanding officer, Major General Phineas Riall, had already set out in the hope of saving the Fort Erie garrison; though, unknown to him, the fort, manned by only two companies, had already fallen.

The successful American force was moving down the river toward Fort George. At Chippawa the two armies came together, their strength closely balanced. Riall made the costly error of assuming he was confronted by a group of poorly trained volunteers from Buffalo; actually they were well trained regulars of the United States Army. Riall was forced to withdraw, but only after about one-third of his men had become casualties. The British counted 148 killed, 321 wounded and 46 missing. The American casualties were 48 killed and 227 wounded.

Merritt arrived at Chippawa in the evening. The fighting had ended, but the bloody toll was all too evident. He was both moved and outraged by what he saw:

> I came up in the evening after the action with a party of the troop; every house was filled with the wounded. I stopped at Street's, and spent a very unpleasant night; many of the officers were lying wounded, groaning with pain. Such was the result of the Battle of Chippawa.

He was critical of Riall who, he thought, should have delayed the action until the arrival of reinforcements which were available at Burlington, two days' travel away. Riall had also failed to make use of available militia:

> It certainly is a very delicate thing to censure a commanding officer, particularly one so popular and brave as General Riall, still, in this case, he acted hastily, neither did he employ all the means in his power.

This was not the only occasion on which Merritt was critical of senior officers. He was not one to simply follow orders blindly. While he was upset by Riall's hasty action, he was frequently frustrated by what he regarded as failure on the part of commanding officers to be more aggressive and take advantage of what he considered to be opportunities for offensive action.

He was, likewise, disillusioned by Major General De Rottenburg, who for a short time assumed military command and the civil administration of the province: "He brought with him a great name, so we expected he would do wonders. In fact he did nothing."

Merritt was quite modest about his own military record. He was mentioned in despatches for his part in an engagement between a part of

Indians and some 600 United States Infantry; but he thought he had received "more credit than I deserved, as I was drawn into it against my will."

The circumstances were that he, with three or four others, was engaged in recovering some medical supplies that had been hidden during a retreat. Almost accidentally they became involved in the battle. The Indians, encouraged by their presence, emerged victorious after killing about fifty Americans and taking others prisoner.

For Merritt the war ended at Lundy's Lane, which has been accurately described as "the bloodiest battle of the war."

Following the engagement at Chippawa, Riall had withdrawn to Fort George and the Americans moved forward occupying Queenston. The British faced a desperate situation. There was a shortage of officers and men, and even those who remained on active duty faced the likelihood of reduced rations because of meagre supplies. A number of the militia had spent considerable time on active duty, resulting in neglect of their farms and they were urgently needed at home if crops were to be saved and the vital food supply harvested.

On the other hand, the Americans at Queenston considered their situation perilous, and they decided to withdraw to Chippawa. Riall was quick to take advantage of the move and on the morning of 25 July 1814, with a force of 1,000 regulars, he moved up the river to Lundy's Lane, a strategic location on the Portage Road near Niagara Falls. The Americans decided to move down the river from Chippawa, reaching Lundy's Lane late in the afternoon. Troops from both sides took up positions. Merritt was with a party that arrived in mid-afternoon.

Riall, mistakenly believing he was outnumbered, ordered a withdrawal; but General Sir Gordon Drummond, arriving on the scene, countermanded the order. Then, between five and six o'clock in the afternoon, the Americans attacked. Riall was an early casualty, and as stretcher bearers carried him off the field they strayed into the American lines and were taken prisoner.

This was typical of what was to happen. In the fading light of evening confusion grew. Artillery pieces changed hands and at times men fell from the musket balls of their comrades. There was attack and counter-attack, with musket fire exchanged at distances as close as ten yards.

The fighting went on for five hours; and then ceased, almost as if by agreement, though there was none. Both sides were exhausted. Men had fought from afternoon to night, without even a drink of water. Many fell from sheer exhaustion and lay on a field littered with the bodies of the dead and wounded and the carcasses of horses. The Americans withdrew. The British lacked the strength to pursue.

Merritt was in the thick of this, his last battle. He later wrote an account:

It was getting dark, so that it was impossible to discover friends from enemies at twenty yards distance. The first regiment of militia, under Major Robinson, coming up at the moment, made a disposition of charging in hopes of retaking General Riall. I was sent to communicate his intention to the troops on the hill to our right. On my return to join my troop I went rather too

21

far to the right, falling in with the enemy's 28 Regiment. It was impossible to make an escape, as I was completely surrounded. A few minutes after firing commenced from our men on the hill. Capt. Clark was taken prisoner about the same time. I was taken prisoner by six fellows who were skulking from the fire which then raged with great fury. This put an end to my expeditions and observations of what was proceeding with out military arrangements. My favourite horse, Hyder Ally, was also taken.

In Merritt's view the British scored a great victory at Lundy's Lane, with the enemy driven from the field. Others have recorded the battle as a draw. The British suffered 800 dead, wounded or prisoner. The American casualties numbered 860.

As a prisoner Merritt was taken to Fort Schlosser, just above the Falls on the American side. There, with others — in all 19 officers and 116 privates — they slept by open fires; many had been more than one night without sleep. the following day they were marched under heavy escort to Buffalo, a distance of 24 miles. Merritt was then sent on parole to Greenbush, Mass.

Officers on parole enjoyed a life considerably different to that associated with prisoners of war in more modern times.

Entries in Merritt's diary told of parties he attended, lengthy rides in the country, participation in games of billiards and cricket. When word came of the British victory at Washington there was a special dinner in celebration.

On Sundays he attended church services and was impressed by the number of attractive young ladies in the congregation. But, despite all this, he found the eight months he spent as a prisoner boring, and he welcomed the ending of hostilities, opening the way for his release.

With his military career over Hamilton Merritt was on the verge of a new life, and in more ways than one. Within days of his release he was married.

Chapter Three

THE CIVILIAN

The bride was Catharine Prendergast, daughter of an American physician, Dr. Jedediah Prendergast. While Merritt's earlier diary entries indicate that he had an eye for the ladies, his feeling for Catharine Prendergast went beyond a casual glance. He had corresponded with her during the war, and, whether or not they were formally engaged, they clearly had an understanding. No sooner had Merritt regained his freedom than he hastened to the Prendergast home at Mayville on Lake Chataugua, in the extreme north-west of New York State. There they were married, 13 March 1815.

Prior to the war Prendergast had moved about a good deal, and for a short time the family resided in Canada, making their home near DeCew Falls. Dr. Prendergast was probably the first civilian medical practicioner in the Niagara District. Until his arrival medical attention was available only from army surgeons, most of whom were reluctant to leave their base to attend civilians. Dr. Prendergast travelled considerable distances making house calls.

On one occasion the Prendergast family was involved in a minor accident when their carriage upset on a hill near DeCew. Hamilton Merritt happened to be nearby and assisted young Catharine from the vehicle. This may have been their first meeting; in any event an affectionate and lasting relationship developed between the two. Their families mixed socially and in later years Hamilton Merritt exchanged extensive correspondence with his father-in-law, for whom he developed a great fondness. Shortly before the outbreak of war the Prendergasts moved back to the United States where Dr. Prendergast became active in politics and was elected to the New York State Legislature. He tried unsuccessfully to induce Merritt to move to the United States.

Following the wedding and a short honeymoon the young couple set off by horseback for their new home in the Niagara District. There Merritt lost little time in establishing himself in business. He had occasion to go to Quebec in connection with army matters, and from there he continued to Montreal and New York to make connections with wholesalers. Goods of all types were in short supply as a result of the war and Merritt, having had a taste of retailing through his earlier partnership with William Chisholm, saw an opportunity to engage in trade.

The journey meant the first separation for the couple and Catharine Merritt went back to Mayville to stay with her parents during her husband's absence. This initiated a pattern that was to become increasingly common as Merritt's interests expanded. Throughout their married life Catharine Merritt, whose health was never robust, spent considerable time with her parents.

The transaction of business in the early 1800s was complicated by difficulties in both communication and transportation. For example, on Merritt's return from his initial business trip the stage coach journey from New York to Buffalo took eight days. Sending mail to New York was a slow and costly procedure. Letters were taken across the Niagara River by ferry and then went on by stage coach at a cost of $4. Correspondence with England could only be exchanged once or twice a year. It was the practice for retailers to buy goods from wholesalers in Montreal and New York, they in turn having imported much of their stock from England.

At Shipman's Corners Merritt purchased 25 acres of land and commenced the construction of a combined residence and business, a sizeable structure directly on the Niagara Road. It later became an inn - the St. Catharines House - and eventually burned down.

Typically he thought and planned on an ambitious scale. He opened retail outlets at Niagara, Queenston and on the Grand River, site of a naval base. Importing books he laid claim to being the first bookseller in the province. He also started a real estate business. And all this within months of his return to civilian life.

Before the war Shipman's Corners had already shown promise of becoming a commerical centre. As early as 1797 Thomas Adams had built the inn which was later taken over by Paul Shipman. He was also the owner of a somewhat rundown mill.

Merritt's commercial ambitions quickly expanded. In 1816 he purchased the Adams property, including the old mill which he immediately undertook to restore. Before the end of the year he was able to advertise timber in any quantity or variety, offered for sale at the mill, or delivered by raft to Niagara. He used the facilities of the saw mill to produce lumber for the construction of a grist mill.

He also began trading in salt - a highly valuable commodity. Small deposits of salt were known to exist in the area and a spring on Merritt's property proved rich in the mineral. During the war salt had become exceedingly scarce and what had once sold for as low as $1 a barrel brought, when it could be had, $10 to $15. Merritt found that by boiling the spring water he could produce a steady supply. One entry in his records showed a shipment of 50 barrels to Port Hope. He also operated a potashery.

At an early stage he was confronted with a problem which, in its solution, was to have tremendous significance within a few years. The level of the Twelve Mile Creek fluctuated widely. In the summer months it sometimes dropped to such a low point that his mills, dependent on water power, could not operate. His neighbours faced the same difficulty.

Before long Merritt entered into partnership with Charles Ingersoll for the general merchandising business. Ingersoll was married to Ann Maria Merritt, Hamilton's sister, and the general store was moved to the Ingersoll residence. An advertisement in THE NIAGARA SPECTATOR indicated the type of business they conducted, announcing the company had

> . . . received an additional supply of Groceries, Cloths, Iron, etc., from Montreal, and will have in a few days a quantity of Tobacco, Cotton, and other American articles from New York- ...Sales are for ready pay, or credit of three months...Salt, Flour and Lumber of every description (including building timber) for sale, all kinds of country produce received in payment and the highest price given for House and Field ashes.

Merritt's approach to business was characteristic. He had a broad outlook and a driving force to achieve his ambitions. He visualized the operation of the general store being integrated with various manufacturing and processing works. But the time was not opportune for such expansion. Business conditions declined sharply in 1816, resulting in low prices and tight credit.

These affected his business. Writing his father-in-law, Dr. Prendergast, in 1818 he said there was plenty of business for his mills and he had an almost exclusive supply of merchandise, in addition to the operation of a distillery and a potashery. But, he added, hard cash was extremely scarce. "It will be a long time before I see the dollars laid out in my buildings and other works."

Here was a new personality. This was no dashing young cavalry officer. This was a deadly serious businessman, desperately trying to balance book when commodities substituted for currency, and simply staying afloat was a difficult task. He faced not only business but also family responsibilities. The Merritt's first child, a son, was born in the autumn of 1816, but died in infancy.

The firm of Merritt and Ingersoll was seriously over-extended with local debts of well over $8,000, largely due to land purchases. In addition some $6,400 was owing wholesalers, and one of these companies finally took legal action to recover an outstanding account of $1,300. By 1819 the partnership faced bankruptcy. Merritt's home and mill, as well as Ingersoll's property had to be mortgaged. Members of the family came to Hamilton's rescue and it became a matter of pride that the indebtedness was eventually cleared and the credit rating restored. The partnership was, however, dissolved.

The fact remained that, within four years of his enthusiastic entry into the business world, Hamilton Merritt had failed financially. A short time later he made a telling diary entry: "I understand no branch of business, having been brought up without any fixed object in view of earning a living." True as this probably was, time was to show that it in no way weakened his self-confidence in tackling business-related enterprises of considerably larger proportion than the operation of a general store at Shipman's Corners.

With time conditions improved, as though signalled by the birth of another son — named Jedediah after his maternal grandfather. He was born 1 June 1820. About the same time Hamilton's father, Thomas, sold his property, and with Dr. Prendergast and Hamilton's uncle — Nehemiah Merritt — provided assistance in re-establishing the business.

Within a short time the records show such activity as a shipment of 300 barrels of flour to Montreal, the revenue being applied against earlier debts. The manufacture of salt was expanded, partly in association with Dr. William Chase, an American who made his home in the district and who became closely associated with Merritt. Control of the mill was regained and Merritt's confidence in his financial ability was bolstered. He was once again launched on a new career in a growing community.

The activities of several church congregations indicated the growth. Adjacent to Merritt's property was a little building occupied by the Church of England (Anglican) which the Merritts attended, and beside it was a cemetery. The Presbyterians of the area held regular services in Shipman's Tavern, under circumstances quite different to those normally associated with early Presbyterianism. The clergyman was described as being dressed in "a showy blue coat, white pantaloons, top boots and spurs." Music was provided by a flute and flageolet. The Methodists met at each others homes. The first regular clergyman in the area was the Rev. Robert Addison, who had been sent to Niagara in 1792 as a missionary sponsored by the Society for the Propagation of the Gospel. He served several Church of England congregations in the district.

By the early 1800s the name St. Catharines — sometimes misspelt St. Catharines — was coming into general use, replacing Shipman's Corners or the Twelve Mile Creek. There is, however, little to support the view of a minority suggesting a connection with the name of Catharine Merritt.

As land in the district was cleared, especially along the creeks above St. Catharines, water was diverted and shortages became more acute. A dependable flow was essential to the continued prosperity of the little community, and particularly to Merritt's enterprises. This led to a dream becoming a reality in the construction of the first Welland Canal, a vital link in what eventually became a navigable 2,342-mile inland waterway. In the early 1800s and before the natural features of what is now the St. Lawrence Seaway constituted the artery which carried Canada's life blood to the Great Lakes and beyond. But those who used the route faced the difficulties and limitations of sections of unnavigable water, the greatest of which were the falls and rapids of the Niagara River.

The only means of overcoming that hurdle was by a slow and arduous land portage. But this was to change. Plans were complete for a man-made waterway — the Erie Canal — linking Lake Erie with the Hudson River, and thus providing a new route for water transport between Lake Erie and the Atlantic Ocean at New York. The first sod for the Erie Canal was turned 4 July 1817.

The importance and probably adverse effect on Canada became of increasing concern. Now it can be seen with even greater clarity. Routing transportation and commerce from Lake Erie west through this new canal could have a devastating effect on Eastern Canada and shape the whole future of the Canadian west. The structure of Canada's economy was at stake.

But this, in 1818, was not the immediate worry of Merritt and his neighbours. They were concerned with an energy crisis. They wanted an irrigation channel that would provide a more dependable supply of water along the route of the Twelve Mile Creek. Their outlook was to very quickly broaden; but it was water power they were interested in when a little party set out on a surveying expedition.

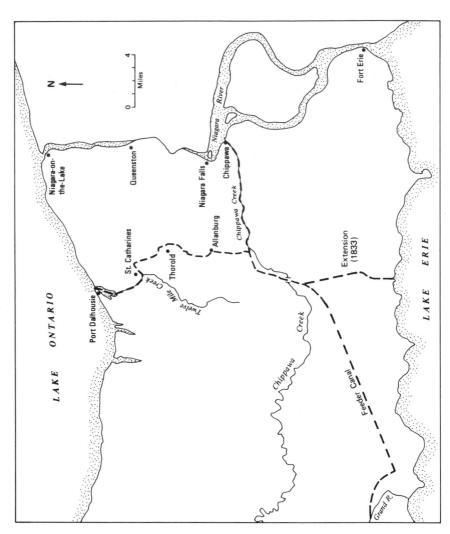

Route of the first Welland Canal

Chapter Four

THE DREAM

On 18 September 1818 three men mounted their horses and set off seeking a new supply of water for their mills. With Merritt were George Keefer and John DeCew, both of whom owned mills which were hampered by fluctuations in the flow of water. Merritt had borrowed a water level from Samuel Becket, another mill owner, and he planned putting to use the rudimentary knowledge of surveying that he had acquired at school.

The three were primarily interested in determing details of a ridge of land which separated the Chippawa or Welland River from the headwaters of the Twelve Mile Creek. They believed that if they could tap the Chippawa they would gain access to a reliable water supply. Merritt was quite familiar with the territory, having ridden over it time and again during the war.

By the end of the day they had estimated the distance between the two waterways at two miles, and their calculation of the contour of the land led them to believe that a cut with a maximum depth of thirty feet would accomplish a connection, diverting Chippawa water into the Twelve.

They were wrong. The fault may have been with the crude level they were using, or with Merritt's limited knowledge of surveying; in any event the true height of the ridge was double their estimate - sixty feet. It may have been a fortunate error; had they realized what was involved they might well have abandoned the scheme then and there. But the survey had convinced them that not only was the plan practical; but it might be expended into a canal that would actually make it possible for ships to pass from one lake to another, opening a new route to the west.

Merritt was anxious to spread the good news and a short time later - 14 October 1818 - he organized a meeting at Niagara to discuss the project and rally support. There was considerable interest and seventy-five citizens signed a petition asking the government to undertake a professional survey. The petition had a highly optimistic note, forecasting great possibilities which were believed to be within easy reach and capable of meeting the threatening challenge of the Erie Canal.

The day spent riding through Niagara forests was already showing results; as Merritt was to comment later: " This trivial affair shews (sic) that stupendous works arise from small beginnings."

This was not the first proposal for a canal. The possibility had been discussed by French officials as early as 1699. In 1793 Robert Hamilton, a Queenston merchant, placed plans for improvements in navigation between the lakes before Governor Simcoe. These provided for a single lock at the rapids below Fort Erie.

Nothing came of this, and in 1799 Hamilton, with Thomas Clark and George Forsyth, petitioned the Legislature for the right to build a road and a canal on the Niagara Portage. Their proposals were embodied in a bill for the House of Assembly. Besides dealing in detail with the road, the document authorized Hamilton and his associates "to make...and to keep in constant repair, a canal or artificial channel, with the necessary locks for raising water to a sufficient height for the easy passage of boats at or near the rapids of Fort Erie."

The Hamilton consortium was to be authorized to collect tolls and the waterway was to be kept open for traffic twenty-four hours a day, except Sundays, Good Friday and Christmas Day. There was considerable opposition to the measure, largely on the ground that it would create too powerful a monopoly. The legislation was dropped and Hamilton died in 1809.

Others thought a canal would eventually prove practicable. Robert Gourlay, in his "Statistical Account", predicted a water link capable of accommodating "vessels sufficient to carry on the whole traffic without unloading, from Quebec to the remotest shores of Lakes Michigan and Superior."

Merritt's proposal was on a far grander scale than that of Hamilton, which was limited to a short canal with a single lock to get around the rapids of the upper Niagara River, forming an appendage to the land portage around Niagara Falls. Merritt, on the other hand, was suggesting a canal that would completely circumvent both the falls and the rapids, making possible complete passage of ships from lake to lake. Sail boats would be pulled through the canal by teams of horses or oxen, using a towpath to be built parallel to the canal. The main rise of the Niagara Escarpment was to be overcome by an incline railway capable of lifting the ships.

The timing was more opportune than in Hamilton's day. The Legislature had authorized a survey of the St. Lawrence River with a view to overcoming the difficulties presented by the rapids there. Legislators were beginning to realize the importance of providing improved navigation facilities in Canadian waters.

The enthusiasm of the Niagara meeting in 1818 was fired by a new idea; but it soon waned. The route proposed — from the Chippawa River to the Twelve Mile Creek , and then into Lake Ontario at the mouth of the creek, later Port Dalhousie — aroused opposition. Business people at the Town of Niagara were quick to see that this would divert traffic which was following the course of the Niagara River, to the benefit of their community. The dispute was to prove long and bitter, shattering friendships and threatening the entire undertaking.

Those living adjacent to the river - the Frontier people - wanted their town to be the Lake Ontario terminus. Merritt's personal stake in the outcome was high. The Twelve Mile Creek route would provide both water and ship access for his mills; the Niagara route would leave him stranded. He used every device he could command to have his way.

A period followed in which little developed, other than surveys, discussion and debates. But the canal was never far from Merritt's mind. He was reminded of it as he rode past the Niagara River returning from a visit to Mrs. Merritt at Mayville. In official circles recognition grew that the project was a matter of "national importance." A commission composed of representatives of the two provinces recognized the very real and immediate threat that the Erie Canal presented. Montreal and Quebec were most vulnerable.

The commission urged that no time be lost in the construction of a navigable waterway in Canada, providing a preferable route and avoiding the heavy losses which would be incurred if traffic were diverted through the Erie Canal. In addition to the commercial importance there was the matter of national defense; memories of the war were still fresh.

The question of whether the project should be undertaken as a public work by the government, or by a private company was a vital issue on which there was remarkably little discussion. The Legislature appeared to assume it would be done by private interests. A committee recommended that encouragement be given to any group prepared to undertake the work, and that steps be taken to enable such a group to acquire the necessary land.

On the other hand, Merritt originally conceived the canal as a government undertaking; this appeared implicit in the petition of 1818. However, events soon changed his mind. A survey by government engineers favoured a route from the Grand River to Burlington, a distance of some fifty miles which was almost double the length of the Twelve Mile Creek route. Despite the length this proposal was favoured by the military, being well back from the frontier. But this was entirely contrary to Merritt's interest and intention. Such a canal would be of no benefit to him personally.

Under these circumstances the organization of a private company, which could choose its own route, became vital; and to this end Merritt gathered some of his friends and supporters at Shipman's Tavern, 22 March 1823. He was impatient at the outcome:

> At the meeting Saturday nothing was effected. Most of the men have narrow minds. They cannot comprehend any measure beyond their daily concerns. They are fearful of some imaginary evil, and do not dwell on the public good. I am, and hope will be wise enough to be adverse to public meetings. Have never seen any good arise from them. We have, however, determined on having the land surveyed, and getting bonds from every person living on the route.

His mind made up he wrote Catharine: "It is my determination...to pursue the object steadily." During the early part of April 1823 he spent a week at Niagara raising funds to finance the new survey. He then went to Niagara Falls and met with an American engineer, Hiram Tibbet, who had been engaged to survey a route for a canal around Niagara Falls on the American side. This possibility naturally added urgency to Merritt's plans.

He arranged for Tibbet's services and personally conducted him over the Twelve Mile Creek route. Things were moving and he wrote Catharine with confidence: "The water of the Chippawa will be down the Twelve in two years." It is hardly surprising that Tibbet's report, after his tour of inspection with Merritt, favoured using the Twelve Mile Creek. He based his estimates on a canal with a draught of four feet and an incline railway at DeCew to lift ships up the Niagara Escarpment. He calculated the cost of the canal at $34,500, with an additional $4,000 to $5,000 for the railway.

At a meeting in June 1823 Merritt was appointed "agent", or general manager, and it was decided to apply for a charter incorporating the Welland Canal Company, with authorized capital of £25,000 — at the prevailing rate of exchange £1 equalled roughly $4. The timetable called for work to start in May 1824 and to be completed within two years.

Not only were these founders of the Welland Canal over-optimistic; they were misinformed. The proposed four-foot draught was quite inadequate. The matter of the route was still in dispute, though Merritt was doing his best to avoid open conflict. Tibbet's cost estimates were wildly inaccurate.

Nevertheless, the Upper Canadian Assembly formally approved the Company's charter on 19 January 1824. The establishment of such a corporation was without precedent in Upper Canada. The Welland Canal Company was in business and a dream was on the way to becoming a reality. But obtaining a charter was to prove the least of the obstacles facing the optimistic little group. As soon as the charter was received a meeting was held at Niagara and a committee — in effect a board of directors — was appointed to promote the sale of shares and press forward with construction. The members were all residents of the area, none of whom bought more than a few shares. Merritt, at the age of thirty-one, was the youngest. The others were:
— George Keefer, member of a Loyalist family that had settled near Thorold where he operated a store, two saw mills and a flour mill; making him one of the district's most important businessmen.
— Thomas Merritt, Hamilton's father.
— George Adams, operator of a mill on the Twelve Mile Creek.
— William Chisholm, merchant at Shipman's Corners.
— Paul Shipman, tavern owner.
— John DeCew, owner of the mill at DeCew Falls.
They were a group of innocents with extremely limited business experience and none at all in major construction. They were completely unaware of the problems to come, which were numerous and complex. The choice of a route was to continue to be a matter of contention, leading to bitter disputes which at times threatened the entire undertaking.

It was originally planned that upbound ships would move by way of the Twelve Mile Creek from Lake Ontario to DeCew Falls. There a double-track incline railway would lift them up the escarpment. They would then proceed by way of a cut channel to the Chippawa or Welland River, and thence to the upper Niagara River and Lake Erie.

This plan was seen as providing both a navigable waterway and assuring a supply of water for the mill owners along the creek. But it would accommodate only small ships, with a maximum draught of four feet, and barges. Some shareholders — particularly those in the United States — considered this inadequate. They argued that if the Welland Canal were to offer effective competition to the Erie Canal it would have to accommodate large vessels. The Erie had a four foot draught. It was decided to double the depth of the Welland to eight feet.

This change required a complete revision of plans. The proposed incline railway could not handle the larger ships and the rise of the escarpment would have to be overcome by additional locks and a rerouting to the east. Instead of only five locks, each 60 by 7 feet, there would be forty locks, 110 by 22 feet.

Moving the route away from DeCew Falls was a disaster for John DeCew, who had been a member of the original survey party and one of the first directors. Like Merritt, his primary concern was a water supply. DeCew, a true pioneer, claimed to have purchased a hundred acres of land from the Indians for a blanket and an axe. There he built a hut, sleeping in a hammock to avoid an infestation of rattlesnakes. From that humble beginning he created a little community with an impressive stone residence that had figured in the War of 1812, as well as a mill and houses for his employees.

But all this depended on the water supply. Rerouting the canal meant that not only was he to be deprived of additional water, but much of the water he already had would be diverted. The little industrial complex he had built was doomed. DeCew became a bitter opponent of both Merritt and the canal.

Disillusioned he sold his property and moved away. Ironically the purchaser of his stone residence was a man who had profited from a canal contract, David Griffiths. Only ruins of the foundation remain.

This revision of plans cost Merritt a friendship; but there were other complications. Even more serious, from his point of view, was the determination of the point at which the canal would reach Lake Ontario. It was essential to his personal interest that the canal pass through what is now St. Catharines to the harbour that was to become Port Dalhousie. This route — and only this route — would service his mills. Despite his oft-proclaimed and doubtless honest concern with the development of a navigation system between the lakes and beyond, his personal interest was his guiding principle. At no point did he hold a large amount of stock in the company and only through support for his mills could he profit.

One group of shareholders had a very different idea. These were the Frontier People who lived in the vicinity of the Town of Niagara. They wanted the canal channelled to the lower Niagara River, utilizing the large natural harbour at what is now Niagara-on-the-Lake.

William Lyon Mackenzie, who was then publishing his newspaper THE COLONIAL ADVOCATE at Queenston, ardently supported this position, predicting serious depreciation in property values at Niagara if the canal followed some other route. Another Niagara newspaper, THE GLEANER, referred to the Twelve Mile Creek as "a strange place" to locate the Lake Ontario harbour.

But to Merritt the route was everything. He wrote:
> Our canal is like money, it required great exertions to get it, and still greater to keep it. The Niagara people and the whole of the frontier have . . . combined to take it away from us and I am determined they shall not have it.

The Niagara route was not the only threat, there was still the longer route — Grand River to Burlington — safe from the reach of American cannons.

And there was still another possibility, a route of which Merritt was well aware, but which he was anxious to keep out of public debate. He made this clear in a strange letter to his father-in-law:
> My whole personal interest in this undertaking is the value that it will attach to my property on the route . . . I am satisfied from the experience already obtained there is a cheaper route than ours — which shall be nameless at present. These circumstances induce me to urge the immediate adoption of this, which once completed sets the matter at rest for ever.

While he was careful not to be specific it seems logical to assume he was thinking of a more direct route from Thorold to Lake Ontario, following generally the course of the present Welland Canal. At an enquiry in 1836 an engineer — Francis Hall — expressed the opinion that such a route would have meant a saving of three or four miles. But his opinion was late, the route had by then been decided in Merritt's favour through an amendment to the charter in 1825 specifying the course to be followed. Some of the shareholders who lived along the Niagara River withdrew their investment, a right defined in the charter. This added to the Company's mounting financial troubles. Not until the fourth canal was built in 1932 was the more direct route followed.

Difficulties of a different nature plagued the route at the upper end. From the point where upbound vessels entered the Niagara River they had to battle a powerful current to Lake Erie. At times windlasses had to be used to assist passage. On other occasions heavily loaded ships were delayed until a favourable wind rose.

It was proposed to overcome these handicaps by means of a new cut and the establishment of a harbour at Gravelly Bay on Lake Erie, later renamed Port Colborne. The estimated cost was $200,000 — an almost impossible financial burden.

There were also serious engineering problems. At first it had been intended to build a tunnel through the ridge which separated the Chippawa River from the Twelve Mile Creek. Major difficulties were experienced in the tunnelling and it was decided to revert to an open cut. This was known as the Deep Cut, and became the centre of construction problems.

The whole undertaking was highly labour-intensive. Before the days of mechanization, it was the period of the pick, shovel and wheelbarrow. The only source of energy was the muscle of men, horses and oxen. As many as 1,000 labourers were employed at one time, yet there were still frequent shortages of workers.

Advertisements offered "common shovellers" up to $15 a month, foremen or overseers were paid $20 to $25, and anyone reporting for work with fifteen good shovellers automatically qualified as an overseer. Men with "two good yokes of oxen and a good stout cart" could earn $25 a month. As for living costs: "good common board and lodging" was available at $1.50 a week.

Contractors were concerned not only with the productivity of their employees, but also with their moral welfare. A list of "Rules and Regulations" posted at the Deep Cut prohibited profanity and gambling, and expressed the wish that, on the Sabbath, employees would "give their attendance at a House of Worship and in no case indulge themselves in drinking or tippling." There was to be no discrimination on religious grounds, and workers were advised at the end of the day's work to "put on suitable clothing to preserve health and at an early hour retire to rest."

The chief source of labour was Irish immigrants, some of whom had worked on the Erie Canal. They were a hardy people, used to agricultural labour and better equipped than most to undertake the back-breaking work. They were also considered less vulnerable to illness, particularly the periodic outbreaks of cholera. Many of the Irish labourers were accompanied by their families and they provided their own shelter, building rough shanties near where they were working and moving from time to time as the job required.

The greatest concentration of labour was at the Deep Cut. There mud was shovelled into sacks and carried on men's backs to the top of the embankment. In some situations it was possible to have wagons haul the excavated material to the top; but as the cut deepened this became increasingly difficult. Oliver Phelps, one of the contractors, told of first using four to six oxen to plow, but later having to increase the number to ten. He had nine or ten such teams working at one time and added, "they have as much as they can do."

The Company offered a prize of £125 for the best suggestion for handling material at the Deep Cut. Phelps won with a scheme that was simple but effective. The key was a wheel mounted on a post at the top of the embankment. This was used as a pulley, around which was a heavy rope with a hook at each end, extending down the slope to the bottom. By this means oxen going down were hitched and provided assistance to wagons ascending. This was as close as construction on the first Welland Canal came to mechanization.

The payroll showed an employee — at one time an eleven-year-old boy — with the intriguing title of "grog man." Water available at some of the work sites was contaminated and dangerous to drink. A pail of whiskey, with a tin dipper, carried by the "grog man" served both as a thirst quencher and a stimulant to weary shovellers.

At times the work was seriously affected by epidemics of cholera. The disease was believed to be carried by immigrants, as well as being caused by a noxious gas — miasma — released through the disturbance of earth, particularly in swampy areas. The appearance of a few cases of cholera was sufficient to cause near-panic and a work stoppage. Rumours of the danger made it difficult to attract labour. A reassuring advertisement seeking labourers stated: "It continues to be very healthy here." Out of 800 labourers only one had died the previous week. Another advertisement emphasized that accommodation and medical attention would be provided for any who became ill — an early form of medicare.

The disease usually struck with sudden and devastating effect; strong men was described as wasting to skeletons, and in some cases succumbing within a few hours. The most serious outbreak in the province occurred in 1832, when, for example, more than 400 of York's 6,000 inhabitants died.

On that occasion Mrs. Merritt went to Mayville, which was considered relatively safe. From Marshville (Wainfleet) Merritt wrote her with a graphic account of developments along the canal:

> Heard that the cholera had commenced its ravages that day at Gravelly Bay. Three deaths. Went to the Bay that evening and found Conrad, a contractor . . . with a man by the name of Henry, working on the lock, and one Ross, a labourer at the same place, was dead, and taken only that morning. On Thursday went through the line with Mr. Lewis, and as no new cases appeared that day the men generally resumed work. Slept at Holmes', Deep Cut. That night Lewis was taken. Lewis was very much alarmed and I could not leave him until Cross arrived about two o'clock. Mr. Fuller had bled him and I gave him two pills of opium; he got better immediately and is now well. Returned to Gravelly Bay that night. We found all who got medical aid and were bled recovered; as it was chiefly among the intemperate. Had hopes of continuing the work, but on reaching Gravelly Bay found Dr. Ellis and Mrs. Boles had taken it . . .
>
> Left for the Dam with a determination to let everyone take their own course — stopping the sale of liquor and providing doctors on the spot . . .
>
> I thank God I am in good health and will take every possible care of myself. Should the disease continue I will go to Mayville next week; if not I will remain until the middle of August.

In his book "The Catholic Church in the Niagara Peninsula, 1626-1895", the Very Rev. Dean W. R. Harris tells of Merritt's personal concern for those who were victims of cholera. Once, on an inspection tour, he noticed a labourer who appeared upset. The foreman explained that the man's wife and two children had cholera and the man, named Dolan, had been sitting up with them all night. Merritt called the man over and told him to go home and look after his family. He instructed the foreman to arrange a doctor at Merritt's expense, and to continue the man's pay until his wife recovered. With the approach of cooler weather the outbreak abated.

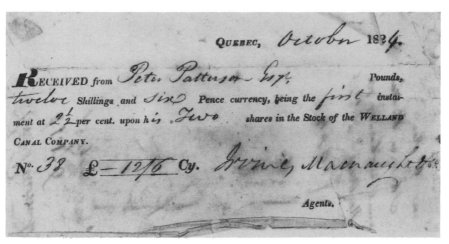

A Welland Canal Share, 1824

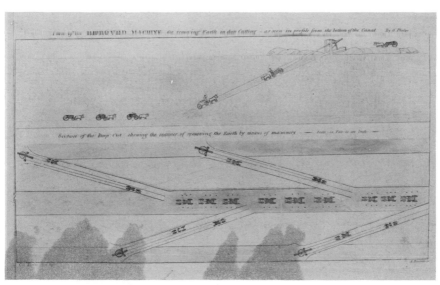

Construction Drawing of first Welland Canal

Chapter Five

THE FINANCIAL TIGHTROPE

Serious as the engineering and construction difficulties were, they were overshadowed by financial problems. At the very beginning it was believed that the whole undertaking could be achieved "at trifling expense", and Merritt proposed capitalizing the company at £25,000. By the time the first ships passed through the canal the cost had exceeded £400,000; and between those two figures was an endless series of crises and maneuvering, narrowly skirting financial disaster.

The Company's original charter authorized capital of £40,000, with shares valued at £12 each. The voting of shareholders was governed by a formula favouring small investors, thus preventing, in theory at least, the concentration of control. The Company was granted the right to expropriate property, subject to arbitrated compensation, and to develop water resources. The government reserved the right to take over the canal after thirty years.

The immediate need confronting the fledgling company was the sale of stock to provide funds. Merritt plunged into the task with great enthusiasm. He had a promotional leaflet printed and circulated more than a thousand copies, sending it to everyone he could think of, from members of the Legislature to local postmasters. Characteristically he became totally immersed in the undertaking. Catharine Merritt, writing a friend, spoke of his being "head over ears in public business, as if he had not enough of his own to attend to."

The canal's supporters were confident that most of the required capital could be raised locally and subscription lists were circulated through the district. Whatever additional support from Lower Canada. But it quickly became obvious that local support was going to be far from adequate; not everyone was enthusiastic about "Merritt's Ditch."

And so Merritt set out for what he hoped would be greener fields. He went first to York where he received a limited response from a few individuals. Proceeding east he paused wherever he could find an audience — Kingston, Gananoque, Cornwall, Montreal, Three Rivers and eventually Quebec. He wrote Catharine that it was "slow, hard work", but he was confident he would succeed. While everyone wished the undertaking well "when it comes to the needful, they keep their hands from paper."

However, he had some success. The Governor General, Lord Dalhousie, purchased shares and his early support is commemorated in the name of the present Lake Ontario community of Port Dalhousie. In total the trip yielded sales of $50,000 in return for travel expenses of $150. While the sales were less than had been hoped for, they were considered sufficient to warrant calling for tenders.

The New York market was seen as the next possible source of funds and it was decided Merritt should go there. This probably marked the first attempt by a Canadian company to sell shares to American investors. Merritt enlisted the assistance of his father-in-law, Dr. Prendergast, who, as a member of the New York State Legislature, had valuable connections and was able to provide introductions.

The idea of the canal quickly caught the interest and imagination of a number of American businessmen. Foremost among them was John Barentse Yates, who became the Company's largest investor and second only to Merritt among the personalities involved in later events.

Yates was the senior member of the New York firm of Yates and McIntyre, the largest lottery operators in the country. Private companies, such as his, conducted lotteries for various purposes and so held large sums of money in the interval between the actual lottery and the final accounting and turning over of funds. The firms supplemented their income by investing this money, usually on a short term basis.

Yates was familiar with the Niagara area. He had fought there with the American troops in the War of 1812 and he had relatives living in the province. He saw great possibilities in the proposed canal operating in conjunction with a channel cut from Oswega, at the eastern end of Lake Ontario, to connect with the Erie Canal near Syracuse, N.Y. This would provide a shorter and faster route than travelling the entire length of the Erie Canal. He promptly bought 600 shares and introduced Merritt to other investors. Throughout the building of the canal it was obvious that Yates' experience as a businessman and his knowledge of financing far exceeded that of everyone else involved.

A century and a half later a street of stately older residences in St. Catharines bears the name of this man, who in his time was the largest lottery operator in the United States, and whose gambling instinct contributed much to the construction of the first Welland Canal.

Merritt's activities in New York attracted the attention of the New York SPECTATOR, whose editor was impressed with Merritt's energy, which he considered uncharacteristic of Canadians. The paper commented:

> We congratulate our friends in that country on the project of improvements before them. The whole scheme or project appears well designed and has been carried on with a degree of energy quite unusual in that country, and we sincerely wish it

may be carried on with the same spirit until completed.

The response was encouraging. New York subscriptions neared the $80,000 mark, leading Merritt to report to Catharine that he had succeeded "far beyond my most sanguine expectations." Among those he had interested were contractors who had worked on the Erie Canal. By mid-November the first contracts were let, and two weeks later — 30 November 1824 — a crowd of 200 attended a sod turning ceremony. Merritt spoke at length, and in glowing terms, of the significance of the event as a step toward navigation on "the greatest extent of inland waters in the whole world." He visualized a flow of traffic to and from the west, coupled with the development of water power; all of which would lead to "a great tide of prosperity."

He attributed delays in the start of construction largely to the disinterest of many of those in authority, and he appealed to local residents to buy shares, expressing the opinion that "it is a rare occurence that measures of such great national importance originate from the administration of government."

George Keefer, who was president of the Welland Canal Company, lifted the first shovel of earth and then others took their turn. After that the official party retired to Beadgersley's Inn, where "numerous toasts were proposed and duly carried." It had been a satisfying day; but it soon became apparent that the Company's sights had to be raised. This meant more capital and Merritt assumed the role of a political lobbyist, spending most of his time in York attempting to rally support from members of the Legislature.

In addition to authority to increase the Company's capital he wanted the route firmly determined. He complained of the legislators: "They do not understand, or scarcely have an idea of canaling." He made a formal presentation to a committee of the Legislature, a new experience and one which he approached with some trepidation but completed with satisfaction. He was gradually becoming embroiled in politics.

Through these activities he established a close relationship with members of the group known as "The Family Compact" — the ultra-conservatives who wielded great influence over the affairs of the province. They were "The Establishment". Prominent among them was Dr. John Strachan, who later became the first Anglican bishop of Toronto. Merritt had a close association with Strachan, who assisted him in the preparation of material and by other means.

Eventually — 13 April 1825 — the amended charter was approved. The changes were sweeping and had considerable impact on events to follow. The authorized capital was increased to £200,000. At the same time the Legislature approved a loan to the Company of £25,000. This was the beginning of a series of loans, grants and stock purchases that were to go on for the next fourteen years as the enterprise moved from one crisis to another.

The number of directors was increased from five to seven and qualifications were added requiring them to be residents of Upper Canada and hold a minimum of twenty shares. This was a significant restriction, without it the Welland Canal would have been controlled from the United States. The formula governing the voting of shareholders was revised to further benefit the small investors, to the detriment of the larger investors, all of whom resided in the United States. Yates, at one point, complained that, despite his heavy involvement, he felt like an outsider.

It was members of the Family Compact who benefitted from the revisions. A number of them had bought shares: John Beverly Robinson, the Attorney-General; Henry John Boulton, Solicitor-General; D'Arcy Boulton, his father; John Henry Dunn, Receiver-General; and William Dunn, president of the Bank of Upper Canada. While Strachan was not a shareholder he continued to give support.

Merritt's courting of the members of the Family Compact was with cause. Hugh G. J. Aitken, a distinguished student of the history of the canal and author of "The Welland Canal Company", has suggested that charter provisions favourable to the Compact was the price that had to be paid in return for their support. Without that assistance the Company would probably not have even obtained its original charter, much less the degree of government aid which it later not only enjoyed but came to depend upon.

Merritt's personal interest in the Compact went beyond this. The members of the group were not all wealthy, nor were they heavy investors in the canal. In most instances they held only twenty shares, the required minimum for a directorship. This represented an investment of about $1,000, which they were able to protect to some degree by their influence in the Legislature. But, apart from their wealth or lack of it, members of the Compact enjoyed a social status that impressed Merritt, who had social ambitions. He aspired to a higher position on the social scale than that of a merchant.

The Company's need for money continued unabated. Yates was asked to raise additional funds in New York; but he was only partially successful. Members of the Legislature were growing skeptical at the repeated requests for assistance, and the voting margin by which such requests were approved narrowed. A point was reached at which the Welland Canal Company, a private corporation, was operating almost entirely on public funds; and even then was surviving only by a hand-to-mouth existence. There was the possibility of aid from the Imperial Government in London in the form of an outright grant; but this was to be subject to negotiation.

The government held the majority of shares, as well as having extended large loans and making outright grants. By 1827 the Company's available funds, even including money owing but not received, amounted to only £39,000. Against this were immediate requirements of £90,000, without any allowance for unexpected expenses. Barring some unforseen development the Company would be bankrupt by mid-1828.

Merritt put forward several suggestions: enlarge the capital stock to £300,000; make a new attempt to sell stock or float another loan in New York; send an agent to England to obtain the Imperial Government loan and sell shares privately. The directors decided Merritt should go to England. It was a desperate attempt to save the canal, and it was not to prove easy.

He left home in late February 1828 and spent the earlier part of March in New York where he arranged for Yates to float another £40,000 loan. He was less successful in other efforts as his diary entries reveal:

Thursday, 13th — Call on Jacob Astor, a German who thinks
well of it.
Friday, 14th — Made a number of attempts in various quarters,
but with very little success.
Saturday, 15th — Having made application to a noted French-
man, German and Quaker — closed with a Jew, agent of
Rothchild.

But the best he could do with Rothchild's agent was to leave an outline describing the canal. He sailed for England, 16 March 1828, on the vessel "Florida". The coast of Ireland was sighted 6 April. The ship docked at Liverpool and Merritt went on to London by stage coach.

He was used to conducting business in familiar surroundings, and most often having his way. In London things were different; he soon became frustrated and impatient, writing his father:

"Of all places this is the most tedious to get through business in a hurry."

He did, however, succeed in obtaining a favourable mention in England's leading newspaper, THE TIMES. He later enjoyed telling how he had made a number of fruitless attempts to see the editor. He finally pleaded for just five minutes of the gentleman's time. Reluctantly this was granted — perhaps as the only means of getting rid of a persistent colonial.

The interview began with the editor pointedly taking out his watch and placing it on the table, Merritt quickly unfolded a map and explained:

Here is Lake Erie. Here is the Falls of Niagara. This is Lake
Ontario. And this is the St. Lawrence and the Atlantic. And here
is the route of the great Welland Canal.

He then folded the map, indicating the conclusion of his presentation, well within the time limit.

Other approaches were less rewarding:

5th — Called upon Chancellor, who appointed Tuesday. Returned and wrote letters to the officials separately.
6th — No interview.
7th — Ditto
8th — Ditto
9th — Called daily and am put off on some pretence or other,
either real or imaginary, all the same to me.

On one occasion he spent half a crown for a seat in the gallery, expecting to see the House of Commons deal with the matter of support for the canal; but again he was disappointed. At last — 24 June — he received a summons to appear before the House of Commons Canada Committee, which was conducting an enquiry into various aspects of political and commercial life in Canada. The members spent considerably more time questioning Merritt on these matters than on the Welland Canal.

Finally he received a favourable response to all his efforts. He was offered the choice of the earlier proposed outright grant, which would have amounted to £16,360, or a loan of £50,000. He took the loan, hoping that it would prove sufficient to enable construction to be completed.

Merritt remained in England for a time, selling what stock he could and seeing as much as possible of the country's industry, in which he took keen interest. The return crossing took a month and he docked at New York 24 September 1828. Near Syracuse, N.Y., on the way home, his stage coach upset and he suffered a double fracture of the thigh which delayed his return and confined him for some time after. Nevertheless, he felt the journey had been a great success, writing Dr. Prendergast: "I am lashed up as effectually as a man in a straight jacket. This has been a damper. Still I have a good appetite and am in good spirits."

Mrs. Merritt met him at Black Rock, near Buffalo, N.Y., and commented: "I never saw Hamilton look so well in all my life." A number of friends and supporters greeted his arrival with great enthusiasm. Appropriately he travelled by boat up the Chippawa River where he was met by a party of horsemen who provided an escort to St. Catharines. That evening there was a great demonstration with lighted flares and the firing of small arms.

But not all the Company's directors shared this enthusiasm for the outcome of his mission. Some felt acceptance of the grant would have been preferable to the loan, arguing that the heavy mortgage involved in the loan would discourage private investors. It was, however, typical of Merritt that, in modern parlance, he decided to "go for broke."

At home, nursing his broken leg, he received encouraging reports. Along the length of the canal there was great activity and the locks were taking shape. However, conditions at the Deep Cut caused concern. There soil conditions were unstable and land slides were becoming an increasing problem.

Then — 9 November 1828 — the Deep Cut collapsed. Not only had the £86,000 spent on the section been largely wasted; but major engineering revisions were going to be required. The depth of the Deep Cut excavation had reached its limit and the required water level could only be attained by increasing the feed from Lake Erie, necessitating a new dam on the Grand River.

Faced with these additional expenses the Company's financial situation deteriorated even further, and was at the same time complicated by the failure of some of the English stock purchasers to meet their payments. The Bank of Upper Canada tightened its already extremely limited line of credit. An appeal had to be made to the Lieutenant-Governor, Sir John Colborne, for a personal loan. He advanced £10,000 on the security of Merritt and Yates.

The situation had become so critical that picks, shovels and wheelbarrows not in actual use were gathered up and sold to raise hard cash. Contractors had to be content with partial payment of money owing them. Time was running out and further government assistance, so desperately needed, was contingent on traffic moving in the 1830 season.

Merritt kept a close eye on the situation, riding twenty-eight miles a day to check on developments. Finally — in September 1829 — water was let in the upper section of the canal. The Grand River Dam, which had been built of trees, brush and gravel, settled several feet. Other faults appeared; but they were patched up. It was decided there would be a formal opening of the canal 24 November 1829.

There was an opening; but with little formality.

Chapter Six

ONTARIO TO ERIE

The stage was set for the opening. The Lieutenant-Governor, Sir John Colborne, was to officiate, accompanied by a detachment of the 71st Regiment, complete with band. Arrangements had been made to assure vessels being on hand to enter Lock One at Port Dalhousie. Merritt rode the length of the canal on a last minute inspection of locks and embankments.

Then the uncertain weather of late November intervened. A storm swept Lake Ontario, making the crossing highly uncomfortable, if not impossible. The directors, most of whom resided in York, decided the opening should be postponed until Spring.

No one was more disappointed than Merritt. The storm soon abated and on 26 November the American schooner "R. H. Boughton" sailed into Port Dalhousie harbour ready to move up the canal. She was followed the next day by the "Annie and Jane" out of York. Her captain, J. Voller, was well prepared. He hoisted an assortment of flags and bunting, including a silk banner reading "The King, God Bless Him."

Merritt decided that — ceremony or no ceremony — the canal should be opened to traffic; and so on the morning of Friday, 27 November 1829, the two little schooners started their upbound passage, the "Annie and Jane" in the lead.

It was not an easy trip. Part of the way the ships used their sails, part way they were hauled by oxen. The temperature had dropped and lock gates were jammed with three inches of ice. Strong headwinds further slowed the passage. But along the banks little clusters of spectators gathered to cheer the mariners on and see history made. Three days later — 30 November — the ships cleared the canal at the Chippawa River and the way was open to Lake Erie. The barrier of Niagara Falls had been overcome. For the first time ships had passed from Lake Ontario to Lake Erie. A new route to the west had been opened.

From Chippawa Merritt despatched a letter to Catharine reporting their safe arrival, despite difficulties: "On the whole we have been successful, and have demonstrated to my satisfaction that a vessel will pass on the canal in twenty-four hours."

On Wednesday — 2 December — the schooners entered Buffalo Harbour to an enthusiastic reception. An artillery unit fired a welcoming salute. The occasion was regarded of such importance that the newspaper REPUBLICAN published a special edition, reporting that, once the ships had docked, "the enterprising projector of the Welland Canal, William Hamilton Merritt. . . and the gentlemen passengers" went to the Eagle Tavern to celebrate their achievement. There they were greeted by many villagers "who called to shake the hands of the navigators of the Deep Cut."

While the participants obviously felt the occasion warranted a celebration, William Lyon Mackenzie, in a sweeping criticism of the canal company a few years later, had a different opinion. He drew attention to an item of £203 in the Company's accounts, which, he said, was mainly for "wine, whiskey, spirits and beef tongues and dinners and poultry", all of which were consumed on "an occasion in which the people were deceived by show."

Mackenzie aside, the important thing was that the mighty Niagara Falls had been overcome and the challenge of the Erie Canal had been met.

The canal through which the schooners passed differed markedly from that originally planned, with the 110 foot locks and eight foot draught double the initial specifications. It was even more remote from the canal now in use. The fourth and present Welland Canal has only seven lift locks, each 858 feet in length, 80 feet in width, with 30 feet of water on the sills and a lift of 48 feet. In addition there is a guard lock, 1,380 feet in length at the Lake Erie end.

The passage of the "Annie and Jane" and "R. H. Boughton" had demonstrated that the canal was practical; but it had done little to relieve the troubles of the Welland Canal Company. Among those who celebrated the opening few realized that the Company, at that moment, had on hand only £152 to meet an indebtedness of £15,467.

It was the end of the season and the real test was to come in 1830. Meanwhile the possible sources of financial help were rapidly drying up.

Another application to the government for a £25,000 loan led to discussions as to whether the undertaking should remain in private hands or be taken over by the government. The legislative committee which dealt with the application proposed increasing the amount of the loan to £200,000, enabling the Company to clear its indebtedness and giving the Province complete control. The Legislature rejected the recommendation and instead approved a loan of £50,000, requiring personal surety of the Company's directors and specifying that the money was to be used for the Port Colborne extension.

In a further effort to raise funds the Company sold some land and water rights to a company formed for the purpose by Yates. The amount involved was $30,000, to be paid over a ten year period and subject to adjustment by penalties imposed on the canal company for interruptions in the water supply. These were so frequent, owing to drainage and repairs, that little revenue resulted.

Most of the Company's immediate debt was money owing contractors, many of whom found themselves in considerable difficulty. A note from one of them to Merritt illustrates the problems some of them faced:

Send by the bearer, my son, one hundred dollars if you can in any way or I shall have to quit work on the Deep Cut, for I have nothing to feed my cattle on after this day and they cannot work without feed and I have three men working for me and their land is advertised for sale for tax and I cannot relieve them without your help.

The whole future of the canal was in jeopardy. Some even suggested that it be abandoned for navigation and used simply as a source of water power. The company was mortgaged to its limit; the Bank of Upper Canada had cut off all credit. To further complicate matters weather conditions in the winter of 1831-2 caused considerable damage.

While traffic in the first two years of operation was disappointing it improved in 1832, partially as a result of the movement of American grain, business Merritt had solicited from Lake Erie ports. He was also engaged in promoting a new project — the Grand River Navigation Company — in the western part of the province.

It was at this stage that he became an active politician, being elected the member from Haldimand in 1832. He regarded this as only a temporary change in his activities, simply providing a means of advancing the interests of the canal project.

Canal matters did not stand still. The government appointed a commission to supervise canal affairs and engaged an eminent American engineer, Benjamin Wright, to advise the commissioners. Wright made several major recommendations, including the construction of stone locks to replace the rotting wooden structures, as well as deeping the feeder canal and harbours. All these improvements were far beyond the capacity of the destitute company, which still owed contractors £12,000. In addition outstanding land claims totalled £8,000 and immediate repairs and maintenance required £6,000.

These developments again brought up the whole issue of public or private ownership. The government's commissioners, in a strongly worded report, made clear their position favouring a government take-over:

The canal ought to become entirely public property. The great navigable communications of the country, like its highways, should belong to the Province, and be entirely and solely subject to the control of the Legislature. Under this impression the Commissioners respectfully suggest that the interest of the private stockholders should be purchased by the Province and that the canal should be rendered in name, as it always has been in fact, and must be in effect, a national concern.

The American shareholders hesitated to support the proposal, fearing they would lose their investment. Yates strongly opposed selling out to the government, a suggestion he found "particularly painful." He was still confident it could remain viable as a private enterprise.

The Board of Directors was in a state of turmoil. John H. Dunn, the president, tendered his resignation, complaining that he had been personally involved beyond his authority. He declared that he wanted to wash his hands of the whole affair, and under no circumstances would he ever again become involved in such an undertaking.

Merritt was well aware that by continuing to seek government assistance the Company was pursuing a course which would inevitably lead to complete government control. The canal company bought back to hydraulic rights held by Yates, thus removing one possible complication should the government decide to buy out the shareholders.

Still Yates remained confident that the company could hang on. He hinted at connections with "a strong European House" which might provide funds; and he urged Merritt to "keep quiet and merely make a general report of prospects." Then an air of further mystery developed. Yates sent Merritt a message: "I cannot write what I wish to propose . . . We have no time to lose — let us now act with promptness and the victory is ours."

Merritt went to New York to consult Yates personally. A short time later the Company formally asked the Lieutenant-Governor on what terms the government's interest in the canal could be purchased. It appeared there were legal complications; but before any action could be taken William Lyon Mackenzie laid a bombshell of charges against the Company.

Mackenzie had long been a critic of the Company, and of Merritt personally, continually complaining of financial mismanagement. At the very beginning he had opposed Merritt's route. It was almost inevitable that the two men should clash; they were completely opposite personalities. Mackenzie, the Reformer, was a bombastic orator, aptly described by William Kilbourn in his biography as "The Firebrand." Mackenzie conducted a running battle with the Family Compact and regarded Merritt in the same light, being highly suspicious of all their motives. At first, when Mackenzie was publishing his COLONIAL ADVOCATE at Queenston, he had an open mind with regard to Merritt, referring to him as a possible candidate in the 1824 election as "well spoken of"; but that opinion was to change.

Of a short wiry build, Mackenzie was completely bald and wore a poorly-fitted flaming red wig, which, on occasion, he would pull off and hurl to the floor to emphasize a point. Such conduct could never be imagined of Merritt, a deadly serious character and a stately figure whose speeches were at times a ponderous collection of uninspiring facts.

As time went by the Welland Canal increasingly became the peg on which Mackenzie hung his attacks on the members of the Compact who, he believed, were personally benefitting from it. Mackenzie's election to the Legislature in 1824 had marked the beginning of a hectic political career. Five times he was expelled from the House; but he retained his popularity with the voters and was regularly returned. One of these occasions brought him in direct conflict with Merritt. In 1833 Mackenzie, having been expelled but re-elected, appeared at the legislative chamber to take his seat. He was accompanied by a large and vocal crowd of supporters who filled all available space, cheering and hissing as the members debated whether the fiery little member should be recognized.

Finally a majority of the members, including Merritt, ruled against him by a margin of four votes. Merritt later said he had intended voting for

First Welland Canal, Port Dalhousie Harbour

Replica of Schooner in Canal

First Welland Canal: St. Catharines - Thorold

Mackenzie's admission, but changed his mind because of the boisterous behaviour of the spectators who had created "a disgraceful scene", remininiscent of the French Revolution. Mackenzie took particular note of Merritt's action and attacked him editorially.

In 1835 Mackenzie, re-established in the Assembly, was named one of the government's nominees on the canal board of directors and he saw a golden opportunity to intensify his campaign. He obtained the Legislature's approval to conduct an examination of the Company's books; and, fancying himself as something of an accountant, he plunged into the task with the enthusiasm and persistence of a terrier. For five months he devoted himself almost entirely to delving into the most minute details of the Company's affairs. He became so excited with what he found that his journalistic instincts overrode his responsibility to report first to the Legislature.

He published three editions of a newspaper he created for the purpose—THE WELLAND CANAL. It contained a whole series of charges against the officers and directors of the Company, with Merritt in the forefront of those accused of various forms of misconduct. Merritt's response was an indignant demand for a full public enquiry to reveal what he claimed to be the falsity of Mackenzie's accusations.

The matter was referred to a special committee of the Legislature which commenced hearings 9 February 1836 and finally reported 13 April. Most of the interval was taken up with Mackenzie's efforts to sustain his charges. Merritt's defence took three days. The printed proceedings ran to 575 pages, and some were unkind enough to suggest that not only was Mackenzie making political capital out of the affair, but he stood to profit financially by holding the contract for printing the proceedings—the longer they were the more he would benefit.

Nevertheless, his charges were serious. At the outset the committee required him to be specific — and he was. He filed a document listing thirty charges. They included improper financial entries, unjustified expense accounts, favouritism in the letting of contracts and in land deals, the misleading of potential investors, missing records, improper efforts to influence the press, negligence leading to the collapse of the Deep Cut and routing of the canal to benefit "certain individuals".

His evidence filled page after page of detail, much of it related to bookkeeping practices which, he maintained, were deliberately designed "with intent to defraud the public and the canal proprietors." He claimed to have found erasures, false entries, misleading reports to the Legislature and alterations in the records.

The committee, in its report, expressed a degree of agreement:

> They (the accounts) have been kept in a very careless, irregular and improper manner, highly discreditable to to a public body, but your committee cannot say that any intentional fraud against the public or the canal proprietors has been brought home to any individual officer of the company, or that any misconduct complained of in this respect is calculated to benefit the individuals connected with the management of the canal.

Mackenzie had pursued the matter of Merritt's expense accounts with great vigour, asserting "some of them such as no gentleman ought to have made." He cited such items as "cutting hair and shaving", "seegars" and "setting razor." he objected to a £25 charge for the use of a horse and the loss of its saddle on the occasion of an inspection tour by the Lieutenant-Governor, Sir John Colborne, at a time, Mackenzie said, when Sir John was "in receipt of £5,000 a year of public money to keep him in horses and saddles." Merritt maintained the entry was in error.

The committee dismissed this part of Mackenzies charges on the ground that such criticism of personal expenses on justified business was "unworthy of remark", and the detail with which Merritt recorded his expenses was itself evidence of his honesty.

But there were irregularities that were "anything but creditable to the company's officers." Two sets of books had been kept, this by order of the Board of Directors. One was in Merritt's possession and the other in the Company's Toronto office. Merritt's somewhat loose method of operation was illustrated in the evidence of a witness with the fascinating name of Love Newlove. He testified that Merritt

. . . has paid me a great deal of money at different times . . . He always paid me whenever and wherever I met him and wanted it. if he had not the money of the Company he paid me with his own.

The committee found there had been favouritism in the letting of contracts, and some of the directors had been improperly involved in contracts connected with the use of water resources.

One of the most serious of Mackenzie's charges was that the canal had been routed "to serve the purposes of interested individuals" — clearly Merritt. The committee agreed that a shorter and more economical route might have been chosen, less beneficial to some individuals; but no specific evidence existed to show that the decision was based on personal profit.

The committee summarized its findings in these terms:

For some years past the affairs of the Company have been conducted in a very loose and unsatisfactory manner, which may have, and no doubt has, originated in their being much cramped for means to carry on the necessary repairs required to keep the canal open; and when your committee takes into consideration the magnitude of the undertaking, and the many unforseen disadvantages the Directors have had to struggle against, they feel inclined to put the most favourable construction upon their general conduct, and to acquit them of any **intentional** abuse of the powers vested in them.

Members of the Legislature obviously were reluctant to condemn those connected with the project. In retrospect it seems only reasonable to recognize that the whole undertaking was without precedent. It had been initiated and carried to completion by a group—and predominantly Merritt — who had no previous engineering experience and extremely limited financial background. Even the professional engineers involved were dealing with unique conditions. Yates was the only person with sophisticated knowledge of finance. He was the professional and the others were amateurs. His operations were beyond their scope.

The miracle was that the canal had been built and was in operation.

Mackenzie had critically described Merritt as "sometimes paymaster, treasurer and secretary, all in one." He had understated the case. Merritt himself outlined his duties in a litany of responsibilities that would frighten any normal person, and which constituted a strong defence for such failings as were demonstrated. This was his job description:

I have to attend the whole line, keep a detail of the proceedings on each job, a copy of all accounts, decide on all plans and specifications of engineers, encourage and alternately censure each contractor, urge them on as well as the Engineer, particularly that part which requires more labour, look out for contractors, find out what different jobs cost to compare the value of excavation, and have my whole mind and attention placed on the work, to answer and attend to various applications, settle disputes, spend as much time talking as working; paying money to various contractors on the line.

Merritt was elated at the outcome of the enquiry. He wrote Catharine: "The farce has ended. And after being tried by our enemies we have been acquitted with credit. Even my political opponents expressed their astonishment."

But the drawn out probe had done nothing to settle the Company's financial difficulties. Rather, Yates felt, it had added to them. Referring to Mackenzie as "the scoundrel", Yates said he might have been able to float a new loan "if so much noise had not been made."

The damage was great. No further government assistance was forthcoming that year. The canal was rapidly deteriorating; the locks were falling apart and other equipment was sadly in need of repair. The 1836 navigation season was scheduled for 184 days; the canal operated only 93 days.

From the very early stages the undertaking had been closely related to two personalities — Merritt and Yates. On 10 July 1836 Yates died. It was a sad ending. His primary interest had been in financial profit; but it developed beyond that. Yet he died disillusioned and bitter. A few months before his death he had written Merritt: "I am tired out and wish I had never seen the canal, or anything connected with it. It has embittereed my life here and there. They must do as they please."

With Yates went any lingering possibility of the canal being preserved as a private enterprise. The financial situation was hopeless. The Company had only £295 on hand to meet immediate obligations which totalled £10,101. The Directors resorted to a legally questionable device — issuing private notes for use as currency. Talk of a new parallel canal being built on the United States side created a new sense of urgency and the shareholders authorized their directors to negotiate with the government for the sale of their shares.

Meanwhile the government converted its loans into shares and increased the Company's capitalization to £597,300, of which the provincial government held £454,500. The sum of £245,000 was allocated for reconstruction, including the building of stone locks. At the same time the Board of Directors was reduced from seven to five, three of whom were government appointees. In effect the government had taken over complete control of the canal.

Then outside developments interfered with the Legislature's plans. Not only was 1837 the year of the abortive rebellion led by William Lyon Mackenzie; it was also the time of a severe economic downturn and only a portion of the proposed new capital became available.

An army engineer described the sad state of the waterway in a report to Lord Durham shortly after he became Governor General in 1838:

> It is quite impossible, in the present state of the work, to ensure the navigation be kept open much longer unless the whole canal be immediately put into an efficient and permanent state of repair . . . If permanent and efficient measures be not adopted without delay, there is great danger this highly important communication will soon become impassable.

At this point a government commission — reporting an average annual loss of L14,000, with little likelihood of improvement — recommended consideration be given to abandoning the canal as far as navigation was concerned and using it only as a source of water power. A horrified Merritt declared: "The abandonment would be a justifiable on public grounds as suicide in a private individual."

The situation represented a serious threat to the shareholders, and those in the United States were particularly concerned about their investment. In 1839 the government introduced and passed legislation providing for the purpose of the privately-held shares by means of debentures, payable in twenty years with interest on a sliding scale of two to six per cent. Back interest to the time of the original investment was to be paid when the income from tolls reached £30,000 a year. There was some delay in receiving approval from the Crown, but the Welland Canal Compensation Bill finally became law as one of the first measures dealt with when the parliament of a United Canada held its first session at Kingston, Ont., in 1841. Not until 1852, however, were shareholders able to collect back interest.

When the legislation for government purchase was adopted Merritt wrote the shareholders advising them of the terms. A short time later he went to New York and met with a group of American shareholders who commissioned him to go to England in an effort to dispose of their shares which, because of the depressed state of the economy, were worth only a fraction of their face value on the open market.

In this connection Merritt wrote Chief Justice Robinson asking for introductions to some influential financial figures in London. The Chief Justice's reply was a curious document, indicating some concern as to Merritt's possible activities as a "stock jobber" — a wheeler and dealer in stocks. Following profuse declarations of admiration concerning Merritt's honesty, Robinson went on to caution that English shareholders should be made aware that by holding the stock they stood to eventually benefit. He appeared to fear that Merritt might take advantage of their ignorance of the circumstances. In any event his concerns were ill-founded. Merritt was unsuccessful even in disposing of the American's shares. The Legislature later amended the legislation to provide six per cent interest throughout, and on that basis the canal became a public work. The Welland Canal Company went out of existence.

Merritt had been relieved of responsibilities which had been his almost exclusive interest and concern for eighteen years. But a new future awaited. He had tasted public life and he liked the flavour. His early prediction of a short political career was forgotten.

Chapter Seven

THE POLITICIAN

It was inevitable that Merritt should become an active politician. His business affairs and a lively interest in the issues of the day had placed him on the fringe of the political scene. When he was only twenty-four he had been fascinated by Robert Gourlay, a man who was to occupy a highly controversial place in Canadian politics. A Scot, Gourlay had come to Canada in the immigration wave of 1817. Shortly after he was the guest of honour at a ball at Shipman's Inn and Catharine Merritt was his partner for the first round of country dances. Gourlay later commanded wide attention through his research into Canadian affairs and his fanning of the flames of discontent among settlers. He was charged with sedition and banished under the terms of an almost forgotten statute.

When the canal was first being promoted there were suggestions that Merritt should seek a seat in the Legislature. Rather he became a lobbyist. By a strange set of circumstances it was in England that he was first invited and had the opportunity to expound his political philosophy. This was in 1828 when he was in London seeking support for the Welland Canal and the Canada Committee of the House of Commons had seized the opportunity to cross-examine him as a person active in the commercial life of the colony. The timing of the enquiry was opportune. The province was emerging as a new country, probing for its identity and seeking to free itself from the outdated restrictions of colonialism. The committee's questions were pointed, as were Merritt's responses.

He was asked to compare the British form of government, which was followed in Canada, to that of the United States. He declared himself strongly in favour of the British system and said this was also the view of the majority of people in the province. He put it in these terms:

We have the full benefit of their democracy without its attendant evils. They are continually electioneering and changing every officer in the state from a governor to a constable, constitution and all.

Religion was a controversial subject in Upper Canada, much of the discussion revolving around the Clergy Reserves — an arrangement by which one-seventh of lands granted was designated for the support of Protestant clergy. This led to a prolonged argument as to which denominations should benefit. The Family Compact took the position that it was the exclusive right of the Church of England (Anglican). Many settlers objected to the effect of church-owned lots, scattered about the country, remaining undeveloped, thus retarding improvements. Merritt told the committee he was personally opposed to the principle of Clergy Reserves.

Later his son Jedediah expressed the opinion that the London experience provided his father with a new and lasting perspective in Canadian politics. He felt that the questioning of the committee members on matters of colonial policy directed his father's attention to Canadian politics under circumstances that provided a more objective view than was possible on Canadian soil.

The suggestion that Merritt should offer himself as a candidate arose again in 1832 when a by-election was called in Haldimand. Yates was among those who urged Merritt to run, feeling that the Legislature would provide a good platform for the promotion of canal affairs. Merritt had a natural interest in Haldimand through his efforts to promote development on the Grand River and he agreed to stand.

This was before the days of the secret ballot. Votes were recorded by declaration and polling lasted several days, in this instance from 30 October to 2 November. Merritt was elected by the narrow margin of nine votes, overcoming what he described as "violent opposition."

Parliament was in session and as soon as he was declared elected he hastened to York to take his seat. He lost no time in demonstrating that he was not going to be content with the role of a silent back-bencher, as a letter to Catharine explained:

I now feel a degree of independence in being equal with those who before could say what they pleased without my having a chance of replying — the situation is new, but I do not feel the embarrassment I expected. I have already broken the ice. The first day I took my seat, made two motions and one speech on admission of articles duty free from U.S.

Nevertheless, he regarded his new political position as something temporary, as he told Dr. Prendergast:

It is my intention, as soon as the Welland Canal question gets disposed of, to leave this business; and, although it is much pleasanter to be in the House than waiting in attendance, I find legislation so tedious I am heartily tired of it, and if I remain in the same way of thinking I will never return again.

Writing his father he described a typical day in political life. He breakfasted at nine o'clock and was in the House an hour later. Sessions frequently opened without a quorum, but to the skeptical Merritt that seemed to make little difference: "I must say a great deal has not yet emanated from their mutual wisdom."

He went on:

About 1 lunch is served in our quarters, which the messenger
keeps in readiness for us, adding a glass of beer, when we go on
with our work until 6, when we proceed to our quarters next to the
Chief Justice's. Beer, whiskey or wine, as you like, for dinner.
Generally retire to a well furnished sitting room, the member
from Haldimand preparing matter for the House. He is well, but
wearing himself out for Upper Canada.

This was the start of an unorthodox and sometimes stormy political
career that was to prove the primary interest for the rest of his life. On his
election he had identified himself as a Tory. His closest relations had been
with members of the Family Compact, and he no doubt felt they were owed a
debt for their support of the canal. But, from his first election through a
period as minister of the government, he made it abundantly clear that he
was more concerned with policies than with parties.

Some of the issues in which he involved himself were related to his
personal interests, others were more general; but as time went on he found
himself increasingly allied with the Reform group, rather than the Tories.
Merritt would probably have subscribed to the proposition that politics is
the art of the possible. His difficulty was that his conception of the possible
frequently went well beyond that of his contemparies.

He became vitally concerned with the need for constitutional changes
in the government of the provinces. In 1838 Lord Durham was appointed
Governor General, charged with trying to correct the conditions which had
led to Machenzie's rebellion. Merritt saw an opportunity to press his ideas
and barely were Durham's trunks unpacked before Merritt was at his door
with a lengthy document outlining suggestions for changes. It was the first
of several such communications. Durham — known as "Radical Jack" —
was open to ideas and with his secretary, Charles Buller, was impressed
with the argument that the cabinet should be responsible to the Assembly,
rather than to the Governor and his advisers — introducing a form of
"Responsible Government."

Merritt wanted to see the two provinces united, maintaining that the
prevailing divided jurisdiction was a great disadvantage to the country. He
drew a comparison with the United States under a single legislative body:

The only effective remedy is union, all other measures are of
secondary consideration. Establish one common object. Upper
Canadians, Lower Canadians, English, Irish and foreigners,
will unite in improving our situation and making a prosperous
country of Canada, and it will allay all party feeling and restore
a proper feeling.

On another occasion he went into detail, criticizing the method of
appointing members of the Legislative Council and urging a more repre-
sentative form of government. He regarded a comparison of conditions in
Canada with those in the United States as "a humiliating spectacle." He
elaborated: "We see every public work in abeyance, public credit annihi-
lated, property valueless, and our only hope rested on the contemplated
change in the present system."

Durham's final report corresponded with these views in a number of respects and it seems not unreasonable to assume that Merritt's representations carried some weight. Durham favoured the union of Upper and Lower Canada, with the expectation that the other provinces would eventually join. He also proposed extending the authority of the elected Assembly, introducing "Responsible Government." Merritt welcomed the report and endorsed it from platforms in the election campaign of 1841.

This election marked the union of the two provinces. Anticipating the English-French conflict which has bedevilled Canadian politics ever since, Merritt realized that more than rhetoric was going to be required to make the partnership work.

He established contact with politicians in Lower Canada with the hope of developing a working relationship. Sensitive to the importance of bilingualism, he suggested the Speaker of the House be from Lower Canada, or at least be fluent in both languages. He afterwards wrote his son — William Hamilton Merritt Jr. — advising him that, were he to choose a career in politics, he should take care to become fluent in French. This, he said, would give him a decided advantage over unilingual opponents. The years have demonstrated the wisdom and lasting value of such advice.

Merritt emerged from the first session of the new united parliament highly optimistic. He felt confidence had been established between the legislators of the two provinces and he saw the dawn of a new period of prosperity. Good feeling expressed between the people of the two languages appeared to assure the stability of the new parliamentary structure.

With the union the Reform movement gained in both strength and credibility; but in 1844 Henry Draper, an opponent of measures directed toward the extension of responsible government, formed the ministry. He invited Merritt to join his cabinet with the office of Inspector-General. Merritt declined, feeling his sympanthy was rather toward Robert Baldwin, leader of the Reform group, who, in opposition to Draper, was pressing for the right of the elected government to make political appointments, regardless of the Imperial Government. This was seen as an essential element of "Responsible Government."

In 1843 a realignment of constituencies had resulted in Merritt's becoming the member for Lincoln. Subsequently Baldwin joined with Louis-Hippolyte Lafontaine to form what became known as the "Great Ministry" (1848-51). Merritt had supported Baldwin in the vote which brought about the defeat of the Draper government; but his earlier enthusiasm had waned. He was becoming skeptical about the practicality of the new form of government. He also had his doubts about the composition of the cabinet Baldwin and Lafontaine were forming, considering those rumoured for appointment to be unrepresentative of the country and dominated by lawyers, for whom Merritt had little love. He wrote Baldwin at great length, putting forward his views on a number of matters and recalling his own political accomplishments. The letter had all the earmarks of an application for a place in the cabinet.

He received a favourable response and was offered the position of President of the Executive Council. After brief hesitation he accepted, somewhat naively assuming that the invitation constituted automatic acceptance of the policies he had been advocating. He wrote Lafontaine:

You have been in possession of the measures I have advocated, viz: the creating of a perpetual fund from the proceeds of public lands for the support of common schools, establishment of district libraries, etc. I consider it (the invitation) equivalent to accepting these measures by the government.

He became President of the Executive Council 15 September 1848. But no sooner had he taken up his new duties than Baldwin wrote him explaining that he would be expected to support the government, regardless of his personal views. Merritt's reply was that he would support only measures which he regarded as being for the good of the country. Nevertheless, he continued as President of the Council, showing a special interest in public works and transportation.

As a cabinet minister he undertook his work with the same intensity he had displayed in other fields. He wrote Catharine that his days started with an early walk and continued until he finished at nine or ten at night. Christmas was spent at Montreal, one of many holidays on which he was absent from his family.

Despite this dedication, he found his duties monotonous and his diary entries were dotted with such notations as "little accomplished" and "nothing done" but there were compensations and he was delighted when it was decided to use revenue from the sale of public lands for educational purposes. The St. Catharines JOURNAL declared this alone would establish Merritt's name in posterity.

Early in 1850 he was appointed Commissioner of Public Works, the position he had always wanted. This was the peak of his political career. No longer was he on the outside, pressing for the development of the St. Lawrence water route; now he was in a position of authority and able to recommend action. He was highly enthusiastic about the future.

Shortly after his appointment he conducted the Governor General, Lord Elgin, and a party of members of parliament on a tour of the reconstructed Welland Canal. They crossed the lake from Toronto by steamer and then travelled by carriage to Thorold, where they boarded another steamer in the canal. His son, Jedediah, described the occasion:

The day was a delightful one, a glorious sunshine lending a charm to the trip which all seemed to enjoy so well. An abundance of refreshments were on board, which it is needless to say were well attended to.

The party divided, some going to Niagara Falls and others to Gravelly Bay (Port Colborne)

... where, in consequence of insufficient accommodation for such a large company, they encamped for the night, and amused themselves with songs, jokes and boisterous merriment, stimulated occasionally by copious libations, so that many were determined not to go home till morning.

Later in the same year Merritt made an extensive tour of the lower St. Lawrence, travelling by steamer and carriage to inspect public works and explore the possibilities for improvements. His report, published as an appendix to the parliamentary Journal for 1851, was regarded as "a masterly analysis of the water transport system."

He proposed various improvements, including the construction of new piers and wharves and the purchase of modern tugs. He was anxious to develop facilities which would enable lake carriers to proceed as far as possible down the St. Lawrence, providing Canadians with employment and business previously enjoyed by ocean vessels which proceeded well up the river.

The government gave his recommendations a cool reception. This treatment was not new to Merritt, who had a firm opinion on several matters not entirely popular in government circles. He was ardently in favour of financial retrenchment, emphasizing the importance of curbing excessive government expenditures which led to increased customs duties and higher taxation which, felt, seriously handicapped Canadian business. He wanted the civil list reduced and maintained some of the pensions being paid former officials were unjustified. He wanted budgets set for each department and a full public disclosure of the country's finances. Complaints of over-government are timeless.

He was overly optimistic in believing that much of the cost of government could be met by revenue from canal tolls. Such additional revenue as might be required should be raised, he thought, through direct taxation, rather than by tariffs. He urged referendums to authorize any increase in the public debt.

Critics pointed to the contradiction between Merritt's emphasis on government economy and his proposals for large expenditures on public works. Some also suggested that many of his policies were directed to the benefit of his milling and other interests.

The breach of his relations with the Baldwin administration widened and finally — 11 February 1851 — he resigned his portfolio. When Parliament resumed in May he rose in his place as a private member to explain his action. It was another lengthy speech. He said no one had ever assumed office with greater expectation; nor left with great disappointment. He once again compared the prosperity which he said was being enjoyed in the United States with the depressed conditions in Canada, attributing the difference to the fiscal policies being followed by the government — "the most expensive on the continent." His hope had been for a reduction in public expenditures and the development of the country's vast resources. Only these could bring prosperity and end the cries for annexation to the United States.

He formally declared himself an independent, free of ties to any party; but it was obvious he was still going to play a role in the political life of the country. In 1860 he became a member of the Legislative Council, a position he held until his death.

He was consistently successful at the polls, never defeated and twice elected by acclamation; yet the political path he trod was far from smooth. From time to time suggestions were made that he benefitted from political skullduggery. He had active and vocal political enemies who on occasion questioned his right to sit, and even his patriotism.

When he was first elected the member from Haldimand there were rumbles of discontent regarding the manner in which the election had been conducted. They died down; but later — in 1840 — an incident indicated someone might be trying to unseat him. Merritt held the office of postmaster at St. Catharines and the Post Office Commission, in an urgent request, raised questions and demanded details as to the revenue received, his expenses and the amount of time he devoted to post office affairs. Merritt's reply was that the entire revenue was used to pay expenses, including the salary of a full-time clerk who handled all the day-to-day business. Merritt said the only benefit he enjoyed was the right to frank his mail. The matter ended there.

A more serious dispute followed his election in 1844. He had defeated George Rykert by a vote of 554 to 405. A group of eleven electors promptly filed a protest, charging that Merritt was ineligible on a number of grounds to qualify as a candidate and that Rykert should be declared the member. Their petition listed their complaints:

—Merritt was technically bankrupt.

—He had failed to file the required "Declaration of Qualifications."

—Several "aliens" had been allowed to vote.

—"Undue influence" had been used on poll clerks to favour Merritt.

—A Board of Works employee had improperly attended a poll and had acted "the part of a partisan" in favour of Merritt.

—"Preachers of the Gospel" had been allowed to vote, contrary to the law.

—"Riotous conduct" had been permited in Wright's Tavern in St. Catharines, interferring with voters exercising their franchise.

The references to Merritt's financial situation were related to a complicated series of some thirty-five legal actions revolving around the leasing of mills in which Merritt had an interest. A formal parliamentary enquiry followed; but this and other charges of the eleven petitioners appear to have been dropped. Instead the investigation centred on an accusation that Merritt was actually an employee of the Department of Public Works, and so could not qualify as a candidate.

A few months prior to the election he had written the Minister of Public Works suggesting that his services might be used to supervise public works, and making it clear that he would expect to be compensated. A short time later he was offered and accepted such a position with the renumeration set at £500 a year. Just before the election he wrote the Minister relinquishing the post and explaining that, as he had never filled the position no formal resignation seemed necessary. Evidence was given before the investigating committee showing he had never applied for nor received any salary.

After hearing all the evidence the committee found itself deadlocked in a tie vote, which the chairman broke in Merritt's favour. The committee reported there was insufficient evidence to support the contention that Merritt was a government employee. Skeptics remained, the Montreal HERALD termed it "a most extraordinary verdict" and a "shamelessly gross instance of twisting fact and law." Party lines had been sharply drawn in the whole affair, even though one of Merritt's colleagues on the government side voted against him. The matter finally died down and Merritt retained his seat.

His status was challenged in a different way during and after the Rebellion of 1837. This was a hectic period in which the Merritt family became deeply embroiled. Word of uprising led by William Lyon Mackenzie reached the Niagara District 6 December 1837. Rumours were rampant, among them was a report that Toronto was besieged by the rebels and an attack on the City Hall was imminent. In the Niagara area there was a flurry of activity in which Merritt was quite naturally involved.

The first reaction was to mobilize the militia and arrange for transportation across the lake. In St. Catharines a party of fifty cavalry was assembled and rode off to Niagara, a three-and-a-half hour journey over muddy roads; and "as they passed every window flew open, handkerchiefs waved." At Niagara it was found that the only available ship could accommodate only twenty horses. Nevertheless, she set sail, only to buffet heavy seas for three hours and then return to port.

When it became evident that there was little danger of the rebels gaining control of Toronto attention turned to organizing provisions, which it was thought might be needed. Merritt was active in this work and the vessel "Jessie Wood" at St. Catharines was loaded with beef, pork and flour.

Young Hamilton Merritt was attending Upper Canada College in Toronto and with some classmates left school to see the excitement. He watched Mackenzie ride by, leading a party of rebels, and "felt a sort of dread for the man." The boys went to see the activity at Government House, the Lieutenant Governor's home, where people were bustling about, some armed and "with melancholy exhibited on every countenance." At the City Hall they saw cannons in place with torches ready for firing. The city's shops were closed.

All this young Merritt found a welcome contrast to the dull business of college. Briefly, with some of his companions, he was held prisoner by a group of rebels; but they escaped unharmed.

The following day the students were dismissed from the college and allowed to return home. There was great excitement in the Merritt household. Mrs. Merritt recorded in her diary:

"Oh what a Sunday we spent. The boys have been busy making cartridges and running bullets. What will another week bring forth for our poor distressed country?"

The worst had passed and Mackenzie was fleeing to the United States, following a route through the Niagara Peninsula. It was a journey of some 125 miles and as he rode along the back roads he saw posters with a proclamation by the Lieutenant Governor, Sir Francis Bond Head, offering a £1,000 reward for his capture. It was inevitble that the fugitive should be seen by a number of people, and to many his face was familiar; yet none gave him away. He rounded the western end of the lake, skirting Ancaster and going on to Smithville. There he turned, as if going to St. Catharines, but actually circled back and took refuge at the home of Samuel Chandler, whom he knew to be a sympathizer. After a rest Chandler joined him, riding to a point near what is now the City of Welland, and then continuing by foot to the Niagara River.

Anticipating Mackenzie's action authorities had attempted to seal the border. Ferry service was curtailed and passengers carefully scrutinized. Other boats that might be used for a crossing were secured or disabled. But Samuel McAfee, a Mackenzie supporter who lived on the river opposite Grand Island, had hidden a boat in his carriage house and it was there that Mackenzie and Chandler were going.

Lord Durham

63

Lord Elgin

64

William Lyon Mackenzie

RIGHT REV. JOHN STRACHAN, D.D.
FIRST BISHOP OF TORONTO. 1839-1867

John Strachan   John Toronto

Bishop Strachan

66

Mackenzie had left Toronto on Thursday, and it was Monday morning when they reached the McAfee farm. Mrs. McAfee prepared breakfast; but just before they sat down Mackenzie spotted a party of dragoons coming down the road. McAfee's boat was hurriedly hauled out and across the road to the water and the three men - Mackenzie, Chandler and McAfee - took off for the island, which was American territory.

Any boat was automatically suspect, and Mrs. McAfee was credited with saving the day by diverting the attention of the soldiers. Mackenzie later maintained that some of the men saw him but turned their heads the other way. Once on United States' soil the little rebel considered himself safe from the Canadian authorities.

In Buffalo there were many sympathetic to the rebel cause. The night after crossing Mackenzie addressed a public meeting, appealing for arms and ammunition. There was an enthusiastic response and suggestions that a force be mobilized to occupy Navy Island, a small area of Canadian territory three miles above the Falls. Mackenzie was not enthusiastic about the idea, but he had started a movement that was hard to check. On 13 December the rebels, who identified themselves as "Patriots", occupied the island. It had been expected some 250 volunteers would be in the party, only twenty-four appeared, though they were later joined by others reaching a maximum of about 200.

Back on Canadian territory Mackenzie declared himself pro tem chairman of a provisional government. He responded to the price placed on his head by offering a £500 reward for the apprehension of Sir Francis Bond Head. He issued a lengthy proclamation attacking the Canadian establishment as "military despots, strangers from Europe" and calling on all Canadians to "rise and throw off the yoke." Volunteers joining his little band were promised 300 acres of the best public land, and this was later supplemented by an offer of $100 in silver, payable in five months. The new Provisional Government was at the moment short of cash and script was issued in the amounts of one and ten dollars. It became known as "Navy Island Money", valuable only as a novelty.

No sooner was the island occupied than the Canadian militia took up a position on the Canadian shore, separated from the island by a narrow channel. Through all the excitement Merritt was determined to play a role - or better still roles. For a short time he rode his horse on guard duty - a replay of his military experience during the way.

Along the length of the river steps were taken to prevent the escape of others. The Niagara River - rather than Toronto - had become the focal point of the uprising. A party of 400 Queen's Rangers crossed from Toronto to Niagara, and from there the commanding officer, Colonel Samuel Jarvis, despatched a letter at midnight Christmas Eve to Alexander Hamilton, the sheriff at Queenston, advising him that the detachment would reach Queenston at 8 a.m. Christmas Day, adding: "we shall expect breakfast prepared and waiting."

Canadian authorities regarded Mackenzie's activities on Navy Island, supported as they were by citizens of Buffalo, as a violation of the United States Neutrality Law. Merritt went to Buffalo in an attempt to have the American authorities intervene; but initially they were hesitant to act. Early in January Merritt attended the opening of parliament in Toronto, and then quickly returned to the Niagara Frontier where the action was. There were sporadic exchanges of fire and Merritt worked with the commander of the militia, Colonel Allan MacNab, in assembling boats for use in a possible invasion of the island. Some were hauled by oxen from as far away as the Welland Canal.

The pressure eased, however, when the Canadian authorities set afire and cut adrift the paddlewheel ship "Caroline" which was being used by the rebels to ferry men and supplies from the American mainland. By mid-January the hopelessness of Mackenzie's adventure was apparent and he abandoned the island. The new republic had collapsed.

The tension lingered with spasmodic outbreaks for the next two years. Well before this Merritt had refused to take the uprising seriously. The first flurry of excitement passed and he dubbed it "The Monkey War", apparently in a disparaging reference to Mackenzie. He wrote his father-in-law: "The rebellion was put down most effectively . . . We have nothing to fear from internal strife."

Despite his deep-rooted antagonism to Mackenzie, Merritt showed a considerable degree of sympathy for some of those who faced charges as a result of having been caught up in the events of this tumultuous period. His attitude left him subject to considerable criticism. As a magistrate, a position he had held since 1817, he was required to deal with some of those who had been arrested. Most of the charges they faced were of a minor nature. Merritt was chosen chairman of a group of magistrates in the area and on his recommendation a policy was adopted of dealing with the prisoners as quickly as possible and then allowing them to return to their homes.

Merritt felt this approach deflated the rebels, though it was in contrast to the stern measures adopted in other areas.

To some this more moderate approach was interpreted as displaying too much sympathy toward those suspected of disloyalty. In a few instances the situation was different and the charges were extremely serious. Two of those charged — Samuel Lount and Peter Matthews — were sentenced to hang. Sympathy for them and their families was widespread. Petitions for their reprieve attracted 10,000 signatures. Merritt helped circulate the petition and personally took the Niagara and Haldimand lists to Toronto for presentation to the Lieutenant Governor, Sir George Arthur. The plea failed and the men were hanged.

Merritt also took a personal interest in the case of Benjamin Wait, a Mackenzie supporter who escaped to the United States and then took part in a foray into Canada. He was caught and sentenced to hang. His wife, Maria, travelled the 700 miles to Quebec, where the sentence was to be carried out, arriving just in time to gain his reprieve. He was, however, ordered transported for life to Van Diemen's Land (Tasmania). Mrs. Wait continued her efforts to obtain his release and Merritt was prominent among those who tried to assist her. Wait eventually escaped and returned to the United States.

After the rebellion a new anti-British movement appeared in the United States. The promoters formed groups known as "Hunters' Lodges", their purpose defined in the oath administered to members:

I promise until death I will attack, combat and help destroy, by all means that my superior may think proper, every power or authority of Royal origin upon this continent; and especially never rest until all tyrants of Britain cease to have any domination or footing whatever in North America.

There were rumours that Merritt had been approached to head a lodge in St. Catharines. He vehemently denied that he ever had any contact with the organization, or that a lodge existed in St. Catharines. Nothing further came of it, and his supporters attributed the whole affair to someone trying to collect a reward as an informer.

Merritt might be described as a "whole politician." Involved as he was in such national issues as transportation and international trade, he was at the same time concerned with a multitude of seemingly less important matters, ranging from libraries to the rights of native people. And while he dealt with those in the highest offices — Lieutenant-Governors, Governors General and Presidents of the United States — he never lost sight of the happenings and concerns of his own constituency.

The Bread Riots of 1842 provide a prime example, when violence broke out along the Welland Canal, caused by unemployment and compounded by bitter rivalry between two factions of Irish labourers. Improvements were planned on the canal and advertisements had been published seeking labour. The response was overwhelming; hundreds — some estimates as high as 4,000 — responded, many accompanied by their families.

A number, originally from the Irish County of Cork, had been employed on the Erie Canal. Others, from the Connaught area of Ireland, had been working on the St. Lawrence. Both these projects were completed. Still others were newly-arrived immigrants. The start of canal work was delayed, and in the meantime the job seekers, with their families, were without food or shelter.

As the tension mounted Merritt, as a magistrate and the member of parliament, asked for the assignment of a military unit to maintain order. When this was not forthcoming he swore in special constables; but this action proved inadequate. What the St. Catharines JOURNAL described as "a scene of most shameful disorder and violence" followed.

In an effort to relieve the situation some road work was authorized; but this only provided employment for about thirty men and it actually added to the disruption. The JOURNAL continued:

All was proceeding apparently quiet enough until Monday morning, when a party of Corkorians from this place repaired to the work and forcibly took possession of it by driving every Connaught man from the ground, and threatening them with instant death, alleging, as a reason, their own expulsion by the Connaughts from the St. Lawrence Canal.

On Tuesday morning, however, a group of Connaughts, about 250 in number, and armed with old fowling pieces, rusty muskets, pistols and shellalies, made a sudden eruption into the village, to the great dismay of the inhabitants, and terror of the few Corkorians remaining in it, who were soon fleeing in all directions, through houses, yards and over fences, to escape the fury of their pursuers which they frequently accomplished, but not without two being injured, one by a blow of a shillaly, and the other by a pistol shot. The home of Mr. Hennegan, innkeeper, was only saved from being demolished through the strenuous efforts of Dr. Lee, Roman Catholic clergyman.

That night a detachment of the Royal Canadian Rifles arrived from Niagara Falls; but rumours of the death of a Cork man led to further trouble the following afternoon. The JOURNAL reported:

About one o'clock they (the Cork men) were seen approaching the village in all their force, shouting and vociferating defiance and death to the Connaughts. They were prevented, however, from entering by the Riflemen, who were formed in two divisions across the street with fixed bayonets and brought to the charge, but which these miserable wretches appeared not the least to regard, and with mad impetuosity seemed to rush upon their very points, with a desperate determination to force a passage at all hazards. There was, at this critical juncture, a few minutes of painful suspense, for had the military been overpowered, no one could have told what fatal consequences would have ensued. On the contrary, had the Rifles been compelled, in self-defence, to use the fatal steel, scores of these infuriated beings would have paid forfeit of their lives for their rash temerity. It was not, however, until the order was given to load with ball cartridges, that they relaxed in their efforts to penetrate the village, but in a few minutes after they commenced a tumultuous retreat across the canal bridge and into adjacent fields. To the indefatigable exertions of Dr. Lee, the promptitude of the magistrates and the vigilance and activity of the troops, it is entirely owing that serious and fatal consequences thus far have not resulted from such lawless proceedings.

An uneasy peace was restored and the resumption of canal work gave employment to a limited number; but the situation remained serious, many still being unemployed and without food. This resulted in the looting of stores, warehouses, mills and ships. One group marched into the village carrying signs which read "Bread or Work" and "Peace and Union, God Save the Queen." They made it clear that if food was not provided they intended taking it by force. The JOURNAL reported:

Mr. Merritt remonstrated with them and pointed out the consequences that would certainly follow such an outrageous violation of the law, and ordered them, as a magistrate, to dispense peaceably, assuring them at the same time that everything that could be done was then in progress for their relief.

His efforts were in vain; the crowd broke into a number of buildings and boarded a ship that was moored in the canal.

Merritt's mill was among the premises looted. Then things quieted down with only occasional outbreaks. One of these resulted in the death of a canal worker, which had a sobering effect, ending the violence. The plight of families in need remained and Merritt's name was at the top of a list of subscribers to a fund for their assistance. He donated £10.

The action was typical. He had fought the rebels in Mackenzie's uprising, and then had tried to assist their families. In the Bread Riots he called out the militia and tried to quell the demonstrations, and then led in organizing help for those involved.

Chapter Eight

TRADER — ENTREPRENEUR

Concern with the day-to-day problems of his constituents and involvement in trade negotiations were to Merritt all parts of the whole — the propersity of the province. Transportation was particularly important. The country, to be economically healthy, required both a market for its products and the means of getting those products to market. By the mid-1800s railways augmented the canal system, but water transportation remained significant in carrying agricultural products, as it had been in the early days of the Welland Canal.

When he was in London in 1842, representing the interests of the Welland Canal shareholders, Merritt used the opportunity to press the case for the admission of Canadian goods to the British market duty free. Later that year he served on a parliamentary committee concerned with free trade, which he strongly favoured. The repeal of the British Corn Laws by stages between 1846 and 1849 precipitated a crisis in the Canadian economy. The legislation had given a preference to Canadian goods, and its removal left Canadian agriculture open to competition from the United States.

Merritt took the position that Canadian interests had been ignored by Britain and, as a result, Canadians were left to make the best bargain they could where they could. As far as he was concerned this meant an attempt to establish reciprocity in trade with the United States. This was the government his ancestors had fought in the Revolutionary War, and he had fought in the War of 1812. But it was also Canada's closest neighbour and potentially her best customer. He argued that Canadian interests could not be protected by high tariffs because of the ease of smuggling. He rejected the contention that a freeing of trade barriers with the United States would lead to Canada's separation from the mother country. Rather, he maintained, a failure to equalize the position of the Canadian farmer with that of his American counterpart would increase the likelihood of such a rupture.

In 1847 Lord Elgin arrived to assume his duties as Governor General. Merritt was almost immediately knocking on his door to make representations pointing out the importance of a new trade relationship with the United States. He suggested a Canadian be sent to Washington where there was concern that reciprocity would be damaging to American manufacturing. Merritt wanted it made clear that the proposal applied only to agricultural products and lumber. Acting on his own he had previously entered into correspondence with a number of individuals in Washington.

Elgin's immediate response was to provide Merritt with a letter of introduction to the charge d'affaires at the British Embassy in Washington. Armed with this Merritt found himself in Washington in 1848, engaged in intensive lobbying at all levels from the President down. Apart from the commercial implications, he was concerned that the unfavourable position Canada was in would provide ammunition for the increasing number of Canadians who were talking about annexation to the United States.

In 1849 a Reciprocity Bill passed the American House of Representatives, but not the Senate. It was one step in what was to prove a lengthy process. Merritt at least had a staunch and sympathetic friend in Elgin, the Governor's correspondence with London clearly reflected Merritt's views and indicated his influence.

On a second lobbying mission to Washington Merritt met President Millard Fillmore, who, in his view, compared unfavourably with President James Polk, whom he had met previously: "As far as his appearance and address went, I was pleased with the President. But he did not enter into business like President Polk . . . Such is the apathy of the public mind respecting Canada that it cannot be aroused."

A complication arose when the Americans asked for fishing rights in Canadian waters as a condition of entering into a reciprocity treaty. Canada's maritime provinces strongly opposed this proposal.

Not until 1854 was the Reciprocity Treaty finally completed, allowing free trade in a number of natural products. The treaty culminated almost nine years of intensive effort in which Merritt played a prominent part. He had raised the matter in parliament time and again, and both there and from public platforms had spoken out in favour of a freeing of trade restrictions. He also wrote a number of articles. Lord Elgin went to Washington to sign the documents for what had become known as "Lord Elgin's Reciprocity Treaty." Merritt, who happened to be in nearby Baltimore at the time, was deeply hurt when he was not even invited to attend the ceremony.

Despite Merritt's pique, Elgin deserves credit for his talent in diplomacy. As his secretary, Laurence Oliphant, wrote, those who opposed the treaty claimed that "it had been floated through on champagne." Without altogether admitting this, Oliphant did add: "there can be no doubt that, in the hands of a skilful diplomatist, that beverage is not without its value."

The treaty, which led to increasingly prosperous times as the result of trade in lumber and grain, remained in effect until 1866 when it was abrogated by the United States.

Merritt's partisan politics have been accurately described as hard to define. The same may be said of his attitude toward politics in general. He had rejected the first suggestions that he take a place in the Legislature, and when he did he considered it only a temporary matter. Yet he remained active in politics for more than thirty years.

At times he was totally immersed in political affairs; at other times he was frustrated by a feeling that he was wasting his time as a politician. Other aspects of his working life were similar; he always wanted and expected more than was within easy reach. In correspondence he expressed the hope that his son William would become a statesman; believing he possessed considerable ability and good judgment. Merritt expressed the opinion that "if he continues to improve without being led into dissipation and vice" he would be successful in politics.

Merritt's consistent success at the polls may be taken as evidence of his popularity. In the 1841 campaign one of his workers wrote him that he had the support of the Mennonites because they considered him "a plain man." Yet, despite these victories, his response to politics swung back and forth like a pendulum.

In 1845 he wrote his father-in-law: "I shall (God willing) retire from public life in a few years." The very next year he was so deeply embroiled in trade policies and the promotion of reciprocity, that he turned his milling interests over to his son Thomas, so that he might devote more time to political matters.

His subsequent frustration was expressed in a letter to his son Jedediah in 1849:

> From all I have seen, and from the experience of legislation gained in thirty years, I find events will take their natural course — you cannot hasten or retard them. I would, therefore, advise my sons, at the same time they advocate their opinions, not to take too prominent a part as to lose valuable time, as I have done.

But by 1851 his son William had launched a political career as a St. Catharines alderman. Merritt wrote him in a letter which expressed his political philosophy and indicated the ambitions he held for his son:

> I see by the JOURNAL that you have commenced your political career; although in a humble capacity, it is a step, and if your mind inclines to leading a public life for the benefit of your fellow men, you ought to be well qualified for the duty; but you will find no sinecure, no easy berth, and can only be attained by unremitting industry and attention, by avoiding all sarcasm and offence, by unremitting attention and a kind word to all, friends and opponents. You must also spend your evenings and most of your time studying the constitution, laws and parliamentary usages of Great Britain and the United States, as well as all proceedings relating to our public improvements and works; and leave all conversation on the subject of eating and drinking to those who have no particular object in view. If you make up your mind to follow this course, I have sufficient confidence in your judgment and perseverance to believe you will make a useful and prominent public man.
>
> If, on the contrary, you think it will occupy too much of your time, or deprive you of that independence of thought and action, which

all public men will be subject to, more or less, and those social opportunities of the conviviality which you appear to enjoy; do not commence it or attempt beyond a temporary locality. Reflect upon it and make up your mind to the course you prefer, as my movements will be guided in a great measure by your decision in continuing or retiring from public life.

In the meantime, as you have undertaken this duty, I would give unremitting attention to it and make yourself master of the state of finance in the Town at once.

Unfortunately the political career of William Hamilton Merritt, Jr., was cut short by a fatal stroke in 1860—an event which had a lasting effect on his father.

Jedediah Merritt wrote in 1852 that his father had adopted an attitude toward political parties of "a plague on both your houses", seeing little to choose between the Grits and the Tories. He felt he could best pursue his many and varied interests by sitting as an independent.

While his primary interest was in transportation, Merritt was active in other fields, with varying success. His chief business activity had been in milling; but there had also been the early purchase of a dilapadated saw mill and its renovation to produce lumber for sale and for the rebuilding of a grist mill.

Merritt came to pride himself on the quality of the flour that came from his mills, and he developed markets as far distant as Montreal, New York and London. In conjunction with his mills he operated ships; not always with profit. One of his vessels carrying 4,000 bushels of wheat, valued at $6,000 was lost on Lake Erie in 1838. The crew was saved. His St. Catharines milling operations eventually ran into difficulties through a leasing arrangement with J. Mittleberger and Company. When that firm faced collapse the court held that Merritt was partly responsible for the outstanding debts. Unable to to meet the obligation he had to seek assistance from his father-in-law.

In addition to the milling facilities at St. Catharines he became a partner in 1834 in the construction of a stone mill, steam-operated, at Port Colborne. His son Thomas later took charge of the family's milling interests and also developed a substantial and profitable business in shipping.

Merritt also had large land holdings. At Port Colborne he purchased 200 acres, had it sub-divided and sold lots. He bought land in the Grand River area and briefly considered moving there. He regarded the Grand River as promising location for development and he promoted and invested in both the Grand River Development Company and the Grand River Navigation Company. Neither succeeded and he suffered considerable losses.

Later he backed his son William in a road construction project; this, coupled with other losses incurred in connection with the Welland Railway, left the family, as Jedediah Merritt put it: "the subjects of financial embarrassment." They were indeed embarrassed; writs were issued and Catharine Merritt had to hurriedly sell her Mayville, N.Y., property to raise funds to save the family home from a sheriff's seizure.

Merritt had a long-standing interest in banking, closely related to his personal affairs; and, indeed, was one of the early advocates of a public banking system. In financing construction of the Welland Canal he had experienced great difficulty obtaining credit, largely owing to the near-monopoly of the privately-owned Bank of Upper Canada. He believed tight credit policies seriously handicapped business generally in Upper Canada. Money was far more readily available in the United States. In the early 1830s Merritt tried unsuccessfully both to have the Bank of Upper Canada establish a branch at St. Catharines and to obtain a charter for the establishment of a new bank there.

He repeatedly introduced a bill in the Legislature for the creation of a provincial bank, and in 1837 it came within one vote of passing. When he revived the measure four years later he pointed out that the private banks were making an annual profit of $2,000,000 and suggested that this, if diverted to a provincially-owned bank, could be used to finance public works. His bill failed and thereupon died. After some twenty years he was, however, successful in obtaining a charter for the Niagara District Bank, of which he became president.

Merritt's attitude toward railway construction was ambivalent. Initially he was opposed, regarding railways as direct competition with canals. Later — the Welland Canal completed and improvements effected on the St. Lawrence — he became a supporter of railways and was active in their promotion. He explained this change of heart in an 1845 letter:

> I have never made any movement, as yet, to forward the construction of railroads because I thought the connection of our great waters the first and most beneficial object to attain — that secured in my judgment, that is the moment to commence our railways.

His new interest was timely. Railway development in Canada had lagged considerably behind that in the United States; and American railways were threatening to divert Canadian business to the United States, particularly in the winter months when navigation was closed. In a sense this was a repetition of the challenge which had been presented by the building of the Erie Canal. The Niagara Peninsula became particularly important in rail development because of its position as a geographic bridge between the two countries.

Probably Merritt's first experience with rail travel in North America was a journey the family made in 1831 to the old family residence on Long Island. They travelled by stage coach, canal steamboat and by rail between Albany and Schenectady, N.Y. The rails were wooden, covered with strips of iron. The coaches were drawn by horses, with stationary engines to pull the coaches up steeper grades.

The first railway in the Niagara District was the Erie and Ontario, which initially operated between Queenston and Chippawa. Application for a charter had been made in 1831 and was opposed by Merritt and others who saw it as a threat to the canal. They succeeded in causing a delay, but the charter was eventually granted in 1839. The Erie and Ontario used wooden rails with horse-drawn coaches. Both passengers and freight were carried, but the line survived only a few years.

In 1836 the Niagara and Detroit Rivers Railroad was formed to construct a line providing a shorter route between Buffalo and Detroit, running through Canada. Merritt became involved and was commissioned to sell stock in the Niagara District. A charter was obtained but difficulties were experienced in financing. When the charter was about to run out, in 1845, Merritt undertook to revive the project.

He went to Boston and arranged for new financial backing, as well as interesting contractors. It was thought possible to build the line within the time limit of the charter; but only by the use of wooden rails, and the company wanted iron rails. An application for an extension or renewal met strong opposition from those who felt the line would benefit only American travellers and would be exposed to the enemy in the event of war, being located close to the border.

It was true that the project was essentially American. The Canadian territory through which the line was to pass, along the north shore of Lake Erie, was too thinly settled to warrant a railway. Merritt, however, saw an advantage to having American traffic move through Canada, making possible the building of a line which would spur Canadian development. His critics suggested that this was another example of what they regarded as Merritt's overly-close connection with American interests. They referred to him as "the Honourable Member from New York."

A prolonged debate followed, participated in by various municipalities anxious to protect their particular interest. At the root of the dispute was competition between the proposed Niagara and Detroit Rivers Railway and the Great Western, to the north. Merritt failed in an effort to bring about a merger of the two companies. Later the Canada Southern Railway took over the route proposed by the Niagara and Detroit.

Although Merritt visualized a railway line extending all the way from the Detroit River to the Atlantic Coast he was also interested in local lines. In 1853 he promoted the Port Dalhousie and Thorold Railway — later the Welland Railway. This was at first aimed to supplement the Welland Canal, enabling passengers and light freight to be moved across the peninsula with less delay than was involved in passage through the locks.

Once again difficulties in raising capital arose; but by 1856 the line was in service between Port Dalhousie and Thorold. Three years later it was extended to Port Colborne. Investors in England, where Merritt went on a stock-selling expedition, provided some backing. Some municipalities, including St. Catharines, also purchased shares. Repercussions followed when the Company failed to show a profit. The St. Catharines Council threatened to withdraw and sell off its stock. The St. Catharines JOURNAL — previously a strong supporter of Merritt — warned:

> There is a fearful day of reckoning at hand for those who have induced municipalities like ours to become gamblers in railroads."

The Company applied for and received permission to increase its capital and Merritt went back to England, spending several months attempting to sell stock; but with little success. Work on the railroad had to be halted because of a shortage of funds. Once more he went overseas in 1859. Business in London delayed him and he thus had the good fortune to miss passage on the new mail-steamer "Hungarian" which foundered with the loss of all on board off Sable Island in February 1860.

Merritt's son William, who was deeply involved in the Welland Railway, also went to England, but was even less successful than his father. William became manager of the railway and the business troubles were held largely responsible for his untimely death at the age of thirty-seven. The Merritt family lost heavily in investment in the Welland Railway, which was eventually purchased by the Grand Trunk Railway.

Merritt also had a connection with the Great Western Railway, whose chief promoter was Sir Allan MacNab of Hamilton. Chartered originally as the London and Gore Railroad, it later built a number of local lines, including one from Hamilton to Niagara Falls. In common with other companies the Great Western had difficulty raising capital and MacNab asked Merritt to undertake the sale of GWR stock in the United States. This he did, also dealing with contractors interested in railway construction.

Merritt may not have ranked as one of Canada's greatest railway builders; but his contribution was significant. His interest in railway expansion played an important part in his promotion of the first suspension bridge across the Niagara River. Catharine Merritt also is credited with sparking her husband's enthusiasm.

The gorge at Niagara Falls was a favourite spot for Merritt family picnics. In the summer of 1844 they went on such an outing, pausing on the way to pick up mail at the St. Catharines post office. Their sons — William and Jedediah — were in Europe and a letter from them, read at the picnic ground, described a bridge they had seen spanning the River Sarren in Switzerland. Catharine speculated aloud that it might be possible to build such a bridge across the river before them.

The idea was not entirely new. There had been earlier discussion of the possibility of a chain suspension bridge at Queenston. River crossings were only possible by ferries located at Niagara, Queenston, Niagara Falls, Chippawa and Fort Erie. Now Merritt's interest was aroused. He enlisted the help of Samuel Woodruff, a friend who was an engineer; and soon he was rallying other support. The unprecedented proposal was to build a structure capable of carrying a locomotive and rail cars. A good many dismissed it jocularly.

Two years later companies had been formed — the International Bridge Company on the United States side and the Niagara Falls Suspension Bridge Company, of which Merritt was president, on the Canadian side. Charters were obtained from the respective governments and a contractor — Charles Ellett of Philadelphia — was engaged. The structure was to be located near the site of the present Lower Bridge.

The first task was to establish contact across the gorge. The assistance of young people was enlisted by offering a $10 prize for the first one to fly a kite across and land it on the opposite bank. The response was enthusiastic, but, despite all the kites flown on the first day, none made it. The second day a youngster named Homan Walsh accomplished the feat and collected the $10—no mean sum in those days. His kite string was used to pull successively heavier lengths of rope and then cable across.

Once a cable of sufficient strength was in place an iron basket with two facing seats was introduced to carry passengers. It was a thrilling trip. The basket dropped by gravity to the bottom of a cable loop hung across the swirling white water; then it was pulled up to the opposite shore by a

Niagara Falls Suspension Bridge

Niagara Falls Suspension Bridge (1855)

hand-operated windlass. The fare for a crossing was one dollar. Neither the nerve-shattering experience nor the charge seemed to deter passengers. During the year the basket was in operation more than 2,000 passengers crossed — among them Merritt who was deeply impressed. On a single day there were 125 passengers, 90 of them women.

The bridge Ellett constructed was a plank affair, eight feet wide and supported by wooden columns on either bank. It could accommodate pedestrians and one-way horse and carriage traffic; but was subject to considerable swaying in strong winds or under heavy loads. In any event it was intended as only a temporary structure — in effect a form of scaffolding for the building of a more substantial structure.

Ellett's bridge opened for traffic in 1849 and was soon showing handsome revenue; but conflict developed between the contractors and the directors. Merritt was among those critical of Ellett's accounting methods and delays in construction. Ellett was fired and a new contractor hired — John Roebling of New Jersey, who was later to gain fame as the builder of the Brooklyn Bridge.

Roebling built a stronger structure, supported by heavier cables which were anchored to stone towers on the opposing banks. It was double-decked structure; carriages and pedestrians using the lower level and trains crossing on tracks above. On 8 March 1855 the 23-ton Great Western Locomotive "London" moved cautiously over the bridge, pulling twenty loaded freight cars. A vital link had been established between railway lines in Canada and those in the United States. The bridge had cost $450,000 and remained in operation for forty-two years, returning a handsome profit to Merritt and others who had invested in what seemed to many an impossible dream.

The bridge proved one of the most successful of the various enterprises in which Merritt was involved. Most often he is remembered only as the canal builder. This effort, coupled with his contribution to rail travel, warranted his being regarded as one of the greatest figures in the history of Canadian transportation.

Donald C. Masters, an eminent Canadian historian, assessed his accomplishments well:

> Merritt's ideas have been consistently misinterpreted and his influence underestimated. His entire career was based on a coherent and feasible system which was calculated, by a programme of improved land communication, to make Canada the avenue of trade between Great Britain and the United States.

Merritt was opposed to these new railway lines being entirely in private hands. He thought railways, as well as other major works, should be in the form of a partnership between government and private interests. He saw the role of private individuals as providing the initiative and part of the capital, the balance being provided by government.

Thus William Hamilton Merritt ranked as one of the greatest promoters of his time. He had a driving passion for personal profit; but a vision that went far beyond.

Chapter Nine

MERRITT — THE MAN

What kind of a person was this man who made such a great contribution to the economic development of Canada? His relationship to his wife and children, the conflict between his personal affairs and his promotion of measures of national importance, his social ambitions and his concern with the most humble of his constituents, reveal a complex personality.

His absences from home and family were frequent and often prolonged. He was one of the most travelled men in Upper Canada, at a time when travel presented many difficulties and hardships. When he was not away attending Parliament he was frequently on business trips to some part of Canada or the United States. Five times he crossed the Atlantic, the first voyage by a sailing vessel that took a month in crossing. In addition to conducting business in England, he visited Scotland and Ireland and travelled on the continent.

On his earlier trips abroad he showed the inquisitiveness of a novice tourist. When he first went to England, landing at Liverpool, he made a point of obtaining an outside seat on the top of the stage coach so that he could see as much of the countryside as possible on the 208 mile journey to London. He was much impressed, though his conception of conditions in England in the early 19th century differed considerably from that which is generally accepted. He wrote that he saw "nothing but peace, plenty, good humour and not an individual who had not good clothing and shoes."

He went on:

> I was ten days in London before I met a drunken person. There is less of this vice in the population of 1,500,000 people in this city than in one of our intelligent villages . . . I have scarcely heard an oath in the whole country . . . Cleanliness and neatness in every cottage is remarkably conspicuous. Noticed but one window not cleaned.

His opinion may have changed later when, out walking with some friends, one of his companions had his pocket picked and lost a gold watch. In any event his enthusiasm for travel waned over the years. On a trip to London in 1842 he wrote Catharine:

> I cannot but remark how changed my feelings are since 1828 — fourteen years. Then I had an inclination to see everything; now I would not give a straw to see anything. I have not been inside a theatre or spent a penny on sightseeing.

If travel abroad was boring, it was still more pleasant than travel in North America, which was an experience in discomfort and endurance. Before the time of railroads people travelled by necessity, not for pleasure. The stage coaches they used varied from little more than lumber wagons with canvas tops and rough benches to gaudily-painted coaches drawn by four spirited horses. The coach had no springs, but was suspended over the wheels by leather straps.

Regardless of the vehicle, journeys were bone-shattering. Corduroy roads, made of logs laid crosswise, were still in use at the middle of the century, and earth and gravel spread in the cracks did little to smooth the ride. One English visitor complained that, sitting on his luggage, he wore out a new pair of trousers during a single journey. Another gave an account of a trip that commenced at Hamilton at 6 p.m. and ended at Niagara at dawn. Several times passengers had to get out to lighten the load or help push the vehicle through the mud. Farmers' fence rails were frequently commandeered to pry coaches out of mud holes.

The habits of many of the drivers was an additional hazard. They usually had a close association with innkeepers along the route. Stops were customary every fifteen or twenty miles to change horses and provide refreshments. Drivers were noted for frequently refreshing themselves rather too well, adding to the speed if not the comfort of the continuing journey. For those on longer trips the inns provided meals of a sort and sleeping accommodation which left still more to be desired. A typical inn might have four bedrooms, each with a double bed with a straw mattress suspended on ropes. Guests were expected to share the bed, quite possibly with a stranger. The beds were frequently dirty and vermin-ridden. Some innkeepers used their ballroom for sleeping accommodations, spreading straw on the floor.

While travelling time varied widely, depending on weather and road conditions, it usually took about twenty hours to go by coach from St. Catharines to York. In the more moderate months a lake crossing could be made in a much shorter time. In winter months, when the roads were frozen, coach travel was at its best; but a thaw could make the roads impassable. On several occasions Merritt spent Christmas separated from his family because travel was impossible.

A journey from Toronto to Montreal normally took about four-and-a-half days, with overnight stops. Merritt, travelling this route, once spent two nights in an open wagon, one of them during a snow storm. When Parliament was meeting in Toronto he tried to get home for weekends, which meant leaving Toronto Friday afternoon and reaching St. Catharines mid-afternoon Saturday.

Accidents were frequent and Merritt had his share. Shortly before his first trip to England he was injured when the coach in which he was riding upset on the Hamilton-St. Catharines road. He was still feeling the effect when he left for New York. On the way home from England, in 1828, there was an accident near Syracuse, N.Y. He suffered a broken leg. In 1837 a sleigh in which he was riding upset on Bay Street in Toronto and he had a rib broken.

The most serious accident, however, was in 1840 involving his buggy being driven by his son Jedediah. He was taking the rector, Rev. James Clarke, to Port Dalhousie for a Sunday afternoon service. It was later suggested that a servant had improperly harnessed the horse, and as they went down the hill to cross the canal the buggy struck the horse and it bolted. Both men were thrown out. Clarke died two days later and young Merritt was bed-ridden for several days.

The absences of her husband and the hazards of travel were not the only worries that faced the constantly ailing Catharine Merritt. The family had its tragedies. Their first two children — a son and a daughter — died in infancy; the boy as the result of a scalding accident. There followed three sons who grew to manhood — Jedediah Prendergast, William Hamilton, Jr., and Thomas Rodman. Their last child — Caroline Penelope, died an infant. Mrs. Merritt also suffered at least one miscarriage.

The trouble did not end there. In 1858 the Merritt's home was destroyed by fire. Two years later their son William died of a stroke.

Catharine Merritt's health, never robust, forced her to pay frequent visits to her parents' home at Mayville, N.Y. She was, however, a women of infinite patience, and by nature more light-hearted than her husband. The couple seldom travelled together, but a rare opportunity came in the early summer of 1849, when Merritt had occasion to go to the United States on government business. The trip was planned well in advance and Catharine had looked forward to it during the winter. In the early spring she had been ill; but, as she wrote, all this was forgotten "in the pleasure anticipated of meeting my husband and journeying with him."

They met at Saratoga, N.Y., and though surprised she was elated. "I expected to see him changed, but not so much; he was so pale and careworn; still I was too happy in beholding him after so long an absence." But even this reunion was cut short. An outbreak of cholera was spreading and Merritt thought she should return home, rather than going on with him to New York and Washington.

Catharine expressed her feelings:

> It was indeed a disappointment, and unexpected, although I try to be prepared for all events. I had come a long way, spent a great deal of money, had been led to anticipate this journey to Washington ever since he went from home last fall.
>
> I thought we would have a quiet time for a tete-a-tete before the bustle of meeting inquisitive neighbours, in the hundreds of miles we would travel together, and now, was about to part without having travelled one — no, not one individual mile together.

Catharine was indeed a long-suffering wife; yet, despite these complications their relationship was strong. Hamilton's frequent letters to his wife were usually short and business-like, with all the warmth of an inter-office memo; but there were exceptions. On one occasion, when she was in Mayville and he in St. Catharines, he wrote: "Dear C.- This place no longer seems like home, you being absent." And on another occasion he confided in his diary: "O Lord, my heart overflows with gratitude when I reflect on the peace of mind and happiness I enjoy in having so worthy a consort."

When the location of the capital was in doubt he expressed the hope that Toronto might be chosen so that it would be convenient for Catharine to join him. A short time later — that being the decision — he rented quarters suitable for the accommodation of both of them. Catharine spent time there and was delighted:

> People ask me how I like Toronto, my answer is very well; and why? Because my husband is there. Still Mr. M. is entirely devoted to his public business, and I must reconcile myself to it as well as I can. Scribble, scribble all the time. I wonder he does not lose his senses.

Catharine took great pleasure in the affairs of her family. Particularly enjoying parties for the young people. Christmas also was a time of great celebrations, despite Hamilton's frequent absence. Families made social calls on each other and the church was profusely decorated with ever-greens.

Merritt was a deeply religious man. At the age of sixteen—while he was studying at Saint John, N.B.—he was confirmed a member of the Church of England. As an adult he attended church regularly and frequently recorded his impressions of the sermon.

In the earlier days both he and his father assisted in conducting services in the little church on the bank of the Twelve Mile Creek. During the War of 1812 the building was pressed into service as a temporary hospital, and later a prolonged dispute took place between the congregation and the government regarding compensation for damages. In 1819 the members had petitioned the Bishop of Quebec, asking him to send "a pious clergyman", to whom they were prepared to pay £50 a year, as well as providing "a comfortable parsonage." Hamilton Merritt, with a £25 donation, headed the subscription list for the building of the parsonage. In 1836 the church burned and was replaced by one on a new site, provided by Merritt in an exchange of land. The new building — St. George's Church — still stands.

Closely related to the religious affairs of the day was the temperance movement. Alcoholism was widespread. Any type of gathering provided an excuse for drinking — barn raising bees, auction sales, weddings, social events and funerals. The harsh quality of much of the liquor sold added to the problem, whiskey was available for as little as 25 cents a gallon. In 1856 St. Catharines, with a population of 6,000, had 51 licensed establishments and an undetermined number of bootleggers.

Anna Jameson, in her book "Winter Studies and Summer Rambles in Canada", 1838, had a little rhyme to describe the drinking habits she observed in the Niagara District:

> Men learn to drink, who never drank before;
> And those who always drank, now drink more.

These conditions led to the rapid growth of the temperance movement, which was strongly supported by the Methodist Church. In Upper Canada some of the earliest temperance societies were formed in the Niagara Peninsula. At a series of meetings in St. Catharines in 1835 some 500 were reported to have pledged themselves to total abstinence. But the pledges did not always stick, the societies' records included such entries as: "requested his name to be taken off as he was to be married this day" and "Expelled" or "broken out."

Merritt was not a teetotaler. He enjoyed a drink, though it would seem with some caution. On one occasion he reported to Catharine: "have not drank two glasses of strong water since my arrival in Montreal and wine only twice."

He hesitated to support total prohibition, rather favouring the moderation of true temperance, and he pleaded for patience with those who found difficulty in breaking long-standing habits. The temperance societies — called by their critics "Cold Water Drinking Societies" — sought total prohibition which was referred to as "The Maine Law." When Merritt declined to take a firm strand the prohibitionists opposed him at the polls. Despite this he was returned in the 1852 election; but in the next election, two years later, he supported the Maine Law.

As time went on Merritt displayed a more ecumenical spirit. He was sympathetic to the Methodists and gave them land for a chapel, even though many Anglicans looked on Methodists with disfavour, considering their evangelistic form of worship to be overly emotional and an exercise of fanatics. When Merritt had been questioned by the Canada Committee of the House of Commons in London he expressed the opinion that the Methodists were the largest denomination in the province, and added: "I think they have done more good than any others."

He frequently demonstrated his religious and moral convictions in a practical manner. Despite the considerable pleasure he derived from mixing in upper social circles and associating with those in power, he frequently showed concern for those lower on the social scale. For example, he objected strongly to the practice of jailing debtors, which he regarded as accomplishing nothing but benefitting lawyers.

He campaigned for some form of tangible recognition for the veterans of the War of 1812; but had to settle for the striking of a special medal.

He spoke out frequently on behalf of the native people, and was rewarded by being adopted by the Cayuga Tribe with the name "Roronounhgowaneh" meaning "Big Feathers."

He showed a keen interest in education and was one of the founders of the Grantham Academy in St. Catharines, claimed to be second only to Upper Canada College in Toronto. His sons received full educational opportunity, studying at Upper Canada College, as well as in England and on the continent. He once suggested to them that they devote some of their spare time to helping educate the servants, considering this to be a reward more valuable than their wages. He argued in the Legislature for funds to establish libraries. With his son Jedediah he was one of the earliest promoters of the systematic preservation of material of historic value.

He showed more than a casual interest in the labourers employed on the canal, most of whom were Irish. On one of his trips abroad he made a point of going to Ireland to learn first-hand something of their background. At the time of the Irish famine in 1847 he organized a fund for the relief of the victims. Yet when canal labourers struck in protest at delays in the payment of their wages, Merritt did not hesitate to go to Montreal to hire replacements as immigrants stepped off the boat.

But the memory he left with the Irish was positive. Dean W. R. Harris wrote of him:

> He was a man of great intellectual power, great force of character, and of a largeness of heart that won him a high place in the affection of Irish Catholics employed on their work. There are those yet living who speak of his charity and liberality with warmth and enthusiasm.

St. Catharines, as a terminal point for what was known as "The Underground Railroad", was the refuge for a number of escaped slaves. Merritt was active in the Refugee Friends Society, formed to assist these people in the 1840s and 1850s. He also donated land for them to build a church.

He sponsored a bill in the Legislature for the relief of Quakers and Mennonites, then subject to penalties for exercising their religious obligation to military service.

On the other hand he was opposed to the Masonic Order. In 1826 considerable excitement was caused by the disappearance of an American, Colonel W. Morgan, the author of a book which purported to be an expose of Freemasonry. Rumour had it that Morgan had been kidnapped by a group of Masons, taken to Fort Niagara and then dropped in Lake Ontario. In the controversy that followed Merritt aligned himself with the anti-Masonic group, and from that time on he opposed all forms of secret societies.

There were those who saw a conflict between Merritt's business practices and the high principles he professed. But Hamilton Merritt's conscience was clear. He believed his worldly possessions were a gift, in trust, of a Divine Providence.

A sermon he heard preached by his friend Archdeacon Strachan confirmed this conviction. The text was: "To him that hath shall be given." In a letter to Catharine, Merritt gave his interpretation of the sermon, which he obviously felt had a personal application:

> Those whom the Almighty has favoured with any peculiar talent, rose to eminence, was entrusted by his fellow men with the control of their property; and if a man of industry, application and honesty, he would continue to increase by commanding the respect and confidence of his fellow men, as well as Divine favour. Urged strongly the absolute necessity of persevering in these qualities; and the moment he deserted them, and gave himself up to sensual and worldly gratification, the Divine favour, as well as the confidence of men, would be taken from him.

The question of the extent to which Merritt's efforts were directed to his personal profit, rather than to the more general welfare, strikes at the very character of the man. Certainly his prodigious efforts in launching the canal, determining the route and pushing it through to completion were intended to benefit his own commercial interests. At a later stage, when it was proposed to enlarge the size of the locks, he arranged to have the first

Great Western Train

Typical Stage Coach

improvements made in the section between his mills and Lake Ontario. The expansion plan stopped at that point because of a shortage of funds.

At times Merritt possessed information which would have made it possible for him to make considerable profit from land deals; but there is no evidence that he took advantage of this. He did become involved in real estate transactions; but these occurred when the canal developments were apparent to all.

Criticized for his involvement in land deals, he offered to sell his holdings for the purchase price plus normal interest.

As to the canal itself, his holdings were not large and he saw no likelihood of their showing a profit for a good many years. He made such a forecast privately; but not to those to whom he was trying to sell shares. He declined an invitation from Yates to participate in the hydraulic company which Yates formed to utilize the canal's water resources.

Lord Elgin — Governor General from 1847 to 1854 — had an opinion on the propriety of Merritt's dealings:

> Merritt is, I think, an honest man, that is to say I do not believe he is actuated by any mean or personal motive in the course which he takes — nor do I conceive that he attempts to deceive others, until he has first succeeded in deceiving himself.
> He is very illogical, however, and like most one idea men, utterly unscrupulous in his mode of grouping together facts and figures when he has a case to be made.

A later observer — M. J. Patton, an authority on early shipping in Canada — put it in these terms: "Like men of his type he sometimes saw so far into the realm of the remotely possible as to make him forget the limitations of the actual."

Merritt lived a strenuous and stressful life, and in his later years the toll began to show. At the same time Catharine's health declined still further. For the last year of her life she was unable to walk. In early 1861 her husband was away on a business trip — this time promoting the St. Lawrence Navigation Company to operate ships directly from the Welland Canal to London — and she wrote him:

> Is it possible that I am here yet? I have lived through another long winter, for what purpose my God only knows. I hope and trust that I will fulfill all his designs toward me, so that I may finish my course with joy.

In an effort to improve her condition she was given galvanic, or mild electrical treatments; but to no avail. Merritt also tried the treatment. A short time later he suffered a stroke which affected his speech and deprived him of the use of one arm. The affliction was blamed on the new galvanic invention.

However, Catharine had her better days and on a winter afternoon in early 1862 she "took the air" in the family carriage. The next day — 10 January — she died.

Catharine's death was a very serious blow to Hamilton, and his health continued to fail. He tried to occupy himself with correspondence; but the characteristic drive was gone. With milder weather it was suggested he seek a change and he decided on a trip to the Atlantic Coast. He stopped for a short time at Brockville, working on still another lengthy paper dealing with inland navigation. Then he went on to Montreal. There he suffered what was described as "an attack of erysipelas in the head." His condition was critical and doctors urged his immediate return to St. Catharines.

He was put aboard the steamer "Champion." On a Sunday morning—5 July 1862—the ship entered the Cornwall Canal moving westward. There William Hamilton Merritt died.

There could hardly have been a more meaningful place for him to end his days. The Cornwall Canal was part of the great inland water route in which the Welland Canal was the key. Largely owing to Merritt's efforts traffic that might otherwise have been going to the United States was moving through Canadian waters. The identity of the Canadian economy had been preserved.

The Merritt family motto is "Praesto et Persto"—"I undertake and persevere." William Hamilton Merritt's life personified that principle and qualified him for the title "The Father of Canadian Transportation."

SOURCES AND REFERENCES

Aitken, Hugh G. J., "The Welland Canal Company", Harvard University Press, 1954.

Berton, Pierre, "The Invasion of Canada", McClelland and Stewart, 1980.

Berton, Pierre, "Flames Across the Border", McClelland and Stewart, 1981.

Cruikshank, Brig.-Gen. E. A., "The Conception, Birth and First Steps of the Welland Canal", Ontario Historical Society, 1925.

FitzGibbon, Mary Agnes, "A Veteran of 1812", William Briggs, 1894.

Green, Ernest, "The Portage Road", Ontario Historical Society, Papers and Records, Vol. XXIII, 1926.

Guillet, Edwin C., "Early Life in Upper Canada", University of Toronto Press, 1933.

Harris, Dean W. R., "The Catholic Church in the Niagara Peninsula", 1895.

Hitsman, J. Mackay, "The Incredible War of 1812", University of Toronto Press, 1965.

Jacobs, Major James Ripley and Glenn Tucker, "The War of 1812", Hawthorn Books, 1969.

Jackson, John and John Burtniak, "Railways in the Niagara Peninsula", Mika Publishing Company, 1978.

Jackson, John, "St. Catharines, Ontario — Its Early Years", Mika Publishing Company, 1978.

Jackson, John and Fred A. Addis, "The Welland Canals", The Welland Canals Foundation, 1982.

Kirby, William, "Annals of Niagara", Macmillan, 1896.

Langstone, Rose W., "Responsible Government in Canada", J. M. Dent and Sons Ltd., 1931

Lindsey, Charles, "The Life and Times of William Lyon Mackenzie", 1862.

Merritt Papers, Public Archives of Canada.

Merritt, J. P., "Biography of William Hamilton Merritt, M.P.", E. S. Leavenworth, 1875.

Merritt, W. H., "Journal of Events, Principally the Detroit and Niagara Frontier During the War of 1812", Public Archives of Canada.

Philpott, Lt.Col., "First and Second Reports on Inland Navigation of the Canadas", Public Archives of Canada.

Report, Select Committee, Upper Canada Assembly, 1836.

Simcoe, Elizabeth Postuma, Diary, edited by Mary Quayle Innis, Macmillan, 1965.

Upper Canada Assembly Journals.

ACKNOWLEDGEMENTS

Thanks are expressed to those who have in various ways assisted with this work, in particular:

—**The St. Catharines Standard** — for its active support in recording the history of the area.

—**Dr. J. J. Talman** of the University of Western Ontario, for his valuable suggestions and advice.

—**Louis J. Cahill; Sheila Wilson** of the St. Catharines Centennial Library; **Arden Phair** of the St. Catharines Historical Museum and **Al Plosz** for their interest, assistance and encouragement.

—**The Ontario Archives** and the **St. Catharines Historical Museum** for access to pictures.

(The accuracy of the material is the sole responsibility of the author.)

Other Stonehouse Publications

Cookbooks:
Down to Earth Family Cooking
Pinch of Pinecones
12 to 1 Habit

Seaway Series:
Best of Ships Along the Seaway
Ten Tales of the Great Lakes
Welland Canal Visitors Guide
The Changing Seaway

General:
Glimpses into our Past, Volume I
Glimpses into our Past, Volume II
Niagara Fruit Barns